I Kissed a Lot of Frogs

But the Prince Hasn't Come

I Kissed a Lot of Frogs

But the Prince Hasn't Come

KATHLEEN HARDAWAY

MOODY PRESS
CHICAGO

Library of Congress Cataloging-in-Publication Data

Hardaway, Kathleen.
  I kissed a lot of frogs, but the prince hasn't come / by Kathleen Hardaway.
    p. cm.
  Includes bibliographical references.
  ISBN 0-8024-3184-4
    1. Single women—Religious life. 2. Christian women—Religious life.
  I. Title.
  BV4596.S5 .H35 2002
  248.8'432—dc21

                                                              2002008356

                    3 5 7 9 10 8 6 4 2

             Printed in the United States of America

This book is dedicated to . . .

Mom, Mary, Jim, Louise, Janie,
and to my extended family—
Thank you all for being a family that
loves unconditionally.
I am truly blessed!

James Andrew Hardaway Sr. (1928–1984).
Dad, I wish you were here to read this.
Your deep devotion to Christ
and your sacrificial love to our family
permeates our hearts forever.

The widows of 9-11-01—
May the Lord's divine power
strengthen you, carry you,
and enable you to walk
through your loss of your husbands.
My prayer is that
He will truly meet your
every need.

About the Author

Kathleen Hardaway is on the staff of Precept Ministries International. She has worked in television broadcasting for seventeen years, and has produced and directed Kay Arthur's nationally syndicated television program "How Can I Live?" Her passion as a speaker is to encourage women to never give up, dream big, and be all that God calls them to be. She has a strong desire to touch as many lives as possible with the Gospel of Jesus Christ through her writing and speaking.

Contents

Foreword

Do princes still come to women, whisk them from their singleness, and carry them to their castles where they live happily ever after—or would that be just a fairy tale?

Princes do come to maidens even today. I could tell you some very precious stories, and they wouldn't be fairy tales. But what does the single woman who would love to be married do until the earthly prince comes? And what if he never shows up? Is there "life" without a man, or is it mere existence—a life of deprivation?

Kathleen has some wonderful insights from the Word of God and from the lives of women of God that will greatly strengthen and encourage you. There is at least one Prince for every woman of God—and all earthly princes pale in His presence.

It is on this premise of truth that Kathleen not only honestly deals with the questions that trouble the hearts of so many single women, but also takes the reader to the surprise gift of singleness—which, when lived with passion, bears fruit rather than a feeling of barrenness.

If you are single and weary of being misunderstood or thought of as an anomaly because you're not married, have never known a man sexually, and may never bear children, you'll find this book extremely helpful and encouraging.

I have known Kathleen for about twenty years and have counted it a great privilege to call her not only a precious friend but also a wonderful, exuberant co-laborer in ministry. Never did I imagine I would have the privilege and opportunity to write the foreword of a book Kathleen would write on singleness. She is typical of so many "I never dreamed this attractive, capable, godly woman would still be single"—that is, until I realized her real Prince has something even bigger for her than He could have accomplished if she had a husband! One of those "bigger" things has to be this book—a book God has sovereignly placed in your hands.

Don't grow weary—the Bridegroom is coming and His reward is with Him!

Kay Arthur
Precept Ministries International
Chattanooga, Tennessee

Acknowledgments

hristie, Cheryl, and Martha, thank you for allowing me to use your life stories in this book. You have impacted my life, and I am sure you will touch countless others.

Elsa Mazon and Cheryl Dunlop, thank you for all your hard work and gifted input to this book.

Kay Arthur, Jan Silvious, Betsy Bird, Dorie Van Stone, Anne Graham Lotz, Beth Moore, Nancy Leigh DeMoss, and Joni Eareckson Tada, God has used all of you mightily in my life. Thank you for giving your lives for the work of the Kingdom. I am forever grateful.

Carolyn Capp, thank you for your part in making this book a reality.

Jan Jeter, thank you for being one of the greatest friends a person could ever have, but more importantly thank you for your selfless devotion to the Lord.

Suzanne Goebel, thank you for being the perfect

coach that every friend needs—you truly are a gifted exhorter.

Shan Alexander and Janet Bales, thank you for using your extraordinary counseling abilities to touch the hearts of women who are now forever changed through your love and encouragement.

To all my other friends, I cannot imagine my life without you. You have walked through the highs and the lows of my life, and loved me through it all. I count it a privilege to be your friend.

O   N   E

A Broken Heart

Has your life turned out like you hoped it would? Do you think possibly you have missed it somewhere along the way? Have you asked yourself the question, "Why am I still single?" Do you wonder when or if you will ever get married?

I cannot begin to imagine how many singles have asked themselves these questions. As these thoughts enter your mind concerning your singleness, please know you are not alone. Forty-seven million American women are currently single—that's more than 44 percent of all adult females.[1] What could possibly be happening?

Divorced, widowed, or never married, regardless of the breakdown, the number of single women continues to climb.

How do you deal with the fact that you are part of this startling statistic? What has happened to our world and our society when it appears that a "match made in heaven" does not seem to be happening like it once did? Has God stopped caring, stopped moving?

I love to read the amazing stories about how God brings couples together. There are numerous stories and books on how God's divine hand brings people together. But does it seem like God has forgotten you? Has He?

I will never forget the night I thought I had possibly found my match . . .

A Dream Come True?

It was the evening of the National Religious Broadcasters Convention's formal banquet. On this exciting night, couples dressed in their finest tuxedos and gowns and walked hand in hand to the banquet hall. I finished putting on my last touch of makeup and glanced one more time into the mirror.

I had grown accustomed to going without a date or a mate to this kind of night. But this night was different—I had plans to meet someone for coffee before the banquet. I straightened my black dinner dress, made sure everything was in place, and thought maybe . . . just maybe . . . I would capture this man's heart. It had been a very long time since I was this excited about meeting someone! As I exited the elevator and entered the lobby of the hotel, I saw him. There he stood, looking as handsome as the first day I met him.

Steve* was waiting for me in front of the hotel lobby's fountain. As I walked toward him, our eyes met, he smiled,

---

* As is true with most of the men in this book, I have changed "Steve's" name to protect his privacy.

I smiled, and once again my heart melted. We said our hellos and made some small talk. He then said, "Make a wish," and gave me a quarter to throw into the fountain. My wish, of course, was, "God, after thirty-eight years of being single, could he possibly be the one?" I threw the quarter into the fountain and we walked across the street to the coffee shop.

He was the perfect gentleman. He said all the right things. He seemed sincere and honest, but most of all he appeared to love the Lord. We had so much in common—both of us worked in Christian television broadcasting; both of our fathers were pastors. His passion was to serve God in whatever capacity he was called to. He had even been to seminary.

As our conversation continued, I thought, *Could Steve be the one God has kept for me all these years?* Many first dates are awkward and uncomfortable, and often I am ready to go home almost before an evening has started. In such instances, I am keenly aware that I will never go out with this man again, much less spend the rest of my life with him. Disappointments in my relationships had become the norm, but this evening seemed very different. We talked and laughed, and I felt incredibly comfortable with him. In many ways, I felt like I had known Steve for years.

It didn't take Steve long before he began asking me more personal questions, and this made me somewhat vulnerable from the start. He said he could not believe I had never been married! He asked more questions about my past relationships. I mentioned that I recently had been hurt by a long-distance relationship, and that I had felt taken advantage of emotionally. I went on to say that I was very tired of the game playing, that if a man was interested in me then he should pursue me, and if not, to please leave me alone.

Steve told me that he would always mean what he said, and he certainly would not play games with me. I knew then he was interested in getting to know me further. I hoped he wouldn't see the excitement I was already beginning to feel. It was rare for me to meet a man who seemed so in love with the Lord.

He walked me back to the hotel and then asked, "Can I write you?" He leaned over and gave me a sweet hug and we said our good-byes. For a brief moment it was like a dream.

In a few days, I received a long, handwritten letter from him. He began by telling me he could not stop thinking about our time together and so he had to write. He went on to say how waiting for a wife all these years had been extremely difficult for him. He only wanted God's choice for him, and that was all that really mattered. He wanted God, his wife, and family to be priorities in his life.

Steve had opened up so freely about his feelings—he had jumped from getting acquainted to talking with me in a very personal way. He was so real, so honest about his life and about being single. He, too, had grown tired of waiting. Steve was thirty-six and had never been married. He was different from many other men I had met. When we talked, it was as if he shared his soul with me, like conversations I have with many of my girlfriends. He came in and won my heart, and I was falling hard.

I was completely smitten with Steve's honesty and deep emotions. After waiting all these years to meet God's man for my life, I began entertaining the thought that it might finally be coming true.

Trusting and waiting on God's best, at times, can be a struggle, and our thinking can be skewed. If we are not careful, we fall into the world's thinking, and the pull to do it man's way seems logical. I had decided in my early twenties that I would walk this single life God's way. I have seen too many women who set out to find husbands their way, only to end up in miserable marriages.

I had also determined that I would give up any pursuit of a man and let God bring the relationships to me. I am convinced that God can bring me a mate, any time, anywhere, in some of the most unlikely places. I certainly wasn't expecting to meet Steve in an elevator in Los Angeles!

I remember his first phone call. We talked into the night. The more we talked the harder I was falling. It was like I was a teenager all over again, excited each time the phone rang. What was happening to me?

Valentine's Day

It was early in our friendship, and I had no idea if Steve would do anything on Valentine's Day. At the start of any relationship, it seems people "play the dance" to see who is going to make the next move. I ran to the mailbox and found Steve had sent me the cutest card. The front of the card had a black-and-white photo of a little boy in a baggy suit and top hat, holding a large bouquet of red roses, smiling from ear to ear.

It was as if I saw Steve standing there holding those flowers. It was a great day! This Valentine's Day was different from many I had spent. This holiday had become painful at times. I knew that, when I went to work, I would see that many women had received flowers from their husbands or boyfriends, and again I would tough it out and act as if it didn't bother me. Deep within our beings we all want to be treated as special and loved; this day was just a reminder that I didn't have that "someone" in my life.

My early years of life had been very different. From grade school through most of my college days, boys and men made me feel very special. I had received chocolates, cards, and a wide variety of flowers, jewelry, and numerous kinds of gifts. All the memories of the past flooded my mind. But on this Valentine's Day, this one little card was more special than any number of flowers or gifts I had ever received. I thought I had finally found the love of my life.

Planning the Visit

A few weeks had passed and Steve began to mention coming to see me. With each new phone conversation, more plans were in motion for his visit. As the days passed, my heart grew more and more full of excitement looking forward to the day I would see Steve again. The date was scheduled and finally it was the week before his visit.

One evening after work, the phone rang. It was Steve, and I was thrilled to hear his voice. He began telling me about his busy week of travel and how tired he was. At that moment I realized that his voice sounded different. The feeling that I had was not a good one. I asked him if he had made his plane reservations for his trip to Chattanooga. He said he had not. I knew then that something was very wrong. I feared the answer to my next question, but asked, "Are you coming?" He sounded extremely different and reserved and said, "No."

After some time of silence, I asked him why not. He said he had prayed about it, and he was just not at peace about coming; he was "not ready to pursue another relationship." It was then that all my staying cool, trying to act like I didn't care, left me . . . and I began to cry.

I had always been able to hide my emotions and never show the men I cared, especially if it was too early in a relationship. This time it was different, and he knew I was very upset. He asked, "Are you all right?" but I could not talk. He kept saying he was sorry, asking if I was OK. I was far from OK. It was as though he had taken a knife and driven it straight into my heart. I could not believe what was happening. What did he mean, he was not ready to pursue another relationship? What in the world had he been doing for the last few months?

The hopes of finally having a husband, having children, building my dream home, were once again a wish and not reality. I believe the pain was so great because the thought of turning thirty-nine and being single overwhelmed me. I thought, *Why, Lord?* Another relationship broken. Our conversation continued, but I knew he was not just talking about the trip. This was good-bye.

After hanging up the phone I went into my living room and fell down on my couch. I could not stop crying. It seemed I cried for hours, and just could not move. All I could think was, *WHY? Why was I so stupid to put so much hope in this relationship?* None of my past relationships had worked out. Why did I think this one would be any different? The thought of remaining single made me angry. What was wrong with me?

What made me different from so many who just meet their mates and get married? Why? Why? Why? For years I constantly reminded myself to guard my heart. Frequently I thought, *Don't get too close, and remember we are only friends. After all, he has never said how he really feels.* I would do anything not to get hurt. Break my will, break my pride, but don't . . . don't . . . break my heart. But it was too late.

It seemed time stood still . . . but the tears kept falling. I felt as if my whole body ached. All I could think of was *Why? God, I have waited for so long. How much longer? What will I do now?*

I battled with little desire of really wanting to go on, but I made my way to bed and cried myself to sleep. It was a very long, miserable night. Who wants to face life or anyone feeling so hurt and in so much pain? Somewhere deep within my soul, I cried out to God and simply said, "Help." God in His supernatural way whispered, "Can you trust Me?"

How do you face life when your dreams are broken?

Proverbs 3:5–8 are verses that I have held onto, believing that He does have the perfect plan for my life. "Trust in the Lord with all your heart and do not lean on your own understanding. In all your ways acknowledge Him, and He will make your paths straight. Do not be wise in your own eyes; fear the Lord and turn away from evil. It will be healing to your body and refreshment to your bones." These verses helped greatly during this difficult time in my life.

Ever since I was a little girl I dreamed of getting married. Watching *Ozzie and Harriet* and *Leave It to Beaver* was part of my childhood, and I believed that someday I would have this same kind of life. Getting married and having a family was what people did—it was my American dream.

I had no problem getting dates; I just needed to grow up and get married. I would dream of that perfect wedding day, knowing I would be madly in love with my husband and live happily ever after. But these idealistic thoughts that a man would fulfill my dreams faded as I began to realize that no human could really give me true happiness.

Through the years, I have observed many marriages, and I have seen that marriage, at best, can be an enormous challenge! The unbelievable amount of heartbreak that occurs in marriages today is overwhelming. But my desire to get married was still very strong.

Marriage for me would be miserable unless I married a godly man; therefore, I have chosen to date only Christian men. God tells me in His Word that I must not be unequally yoked (2 Corinthians 6:14 KJV) and, since dating leads to marriage, dating an unbeliever is not an option. Christ is my life. What would I have in common with an unbeliever? I believe, for now, God has another calling for my life, and I must trust Him.

Broken Relationships

Through the years I had grown extremely tired of all the broken relationships. The men in my life were not always the ones who decided to end a courtship. I cannot count the number of men I have tried with everything in me to love— but hard as I tried, I just couldn't love them. Funny . . . trying to love someone is something I would not suggest doing, but there were times I began to think that maybe I was not giving a man a chance. Getting to know the opposite sex in hopes that someday it may turn into a lifetime commitment of marriage can certainly have its challenges.

There are a number of good Christian books about dating, but there are no easy answers to how and when God will bring you a mate. God chooses to work differently in each life. If you trust and obey God, you can walk in confidence that He knows what is best for your life, whether He brings you a husband or not. Remember that all of your relationships should bring honor to Christ.

For some, it has happened almost like clockwork. They prayed, they waited on God, and He brought them their mates. You may be in this waiting period. If you are one who is eagerly waiting to get married, I encourage you to keep praying and trusting God. We must be careful, as many "experts" would give us a list of pat answers on the subject of finding a mate. Certainly there are good guidelines to follow in dating. But what if you have dated according to the best standards and all His precepts and you're still single?

I want to encourage you that if you are not married, this does not mean there is anything wrong with you! For more than twenty years, I have simply gotten to know men in God-honoring ways by going to dinner, to a movie, for walks together—but still have no husband.

The older you are, the longer you remain single, the more likely it is that you have experienced some broken relationships. It seems the hurt of each relationship builds upon the last one. It is not as though dating is a large part of my life, but I am forty-four years old as I write this book, and it has been a long journey. I believe this is why Steve's pursing me so strongly and then breaking it off was so overwhelming. I had become exhausted with the emotional ups and downs that come from broken friendships with men. I wanted to just give up.

I felt hurt, alone, and emotionally overwhelmed. Have you ever felt that way? Broken relationships can seem devastating. I was not looking for anyone when I met Steve. But he showed up out of nowhere, instantly pursuing me. A nice looking, godly man who is working in Christian ministry is not exactly the kind of man I run from! My expectations were high, which made the fall so hard.

God allows suffering in our lives for a reason, so I must trust His Word when He says to "consider it all joy . . . when you encounter various trials, knowing that the testing of your faith produces endurance. And let endurance have its perfect result, so that you may be perfect and complete, lacking in nothing" (James 1:2–4).

Real Faith

Faith is a word that is used by many, but how real is it? Often faith is not evident in our lives until we have to walk through some very dark and lonely places. After Steve, every ounce of my being wanted to stay angry, continue with my pity parties, and eat everything in sight.

It seems the world says that sex, relationships, and marriage are the only ways to be happy. The majority of commercials, billboards, and movies tell us that romance gives us real happiness. I continued to battle thoughts of never having this romance and a lifetime-committed relationship. Just seeing couples walking hand in hand would sometimes pierce my heart and bring tears.

The days passed, and gradually the biblical truths I had studied over the years began to give me hope again. The underlying theme for my existence came down to my faith. God never said that life would be easy, but He did say, "For I know the plans I have for you . . . plans to prosper you and not to harm you, plans to give you hope and a future" (Jeremiah 29:11 NIV). I held on to this truth.

Broken dreams . . . we all have them. But Jesus intends for me to have a life of joy despite my circumstances, a life of peace despite the storms, a life that is complete . . . though single.

NOTE

1. U.S. Census Bureau, "Marital Status of People by Age, Sex, Personal Earnings, Race, and Hispanic Origin" (Table A1), March 2000.

T W O

Bitter or Better

In the face of life's disappointments, what do you do? Do you have friends who encourage you during the difficult periods of your life? I am blessed to have friends who always seem to know just what to say at just the right time.

Get a True Friend

A few weeks had passed when a friend saw the pain in my eyes. She asked, "Are you all right?" We had dinner that evening. As I told her about Steve, her compassion was real, and it made a difference. After talking several hours, she came back to the one question that I had to face: Did I trust God or not?

She then gave me the book *Fix Your Eyes on Jesus*, by Anne Ortlund. This was the perfect book to help me begin to walk this difficult road with renewed confidence that God has a plan and a purpose for my life and that He cares deeply about the pain I feel. When I began to look outside myself, beyond this world, and to look instead on eternal things, my heart began to heal. I learned that it is easy to fix our hope on our circumstances, only to end up miserable and unhappy. We can spend a lifetime hoping our circumstances will make us happy, but when it happens it's only temporary.

Godly advice from friends may not be what you want to hear. But if they are pointing you to the truths of God's Word, be grateful for those friends! Godly friends have played a major role in my walking this life of singleness. You may have experienced a number of broken relationships and can relate to the pain that it causes, but if your friends bombard you with worldly advice, watch out. Ask God for Christian friends, those who want your highest good—not those who will do anything just to help get you married.

It seems the topic of many women's conversations is relationships. Have you ever gone out to dinner with friends and thought, *Will we make it through the evening without talking about men or diets?* I'm not sure which one will get the majority of the discussion, but it is usually a pretty close race! If you surround yourself with friends who are only looking for husbands and this is the center of your conversations and thoughts, be careful. Why? Your focus becomes "me" centered. Then, when your friends have relationships and you don't, you can easily begin to feel depressed and more alone than ever in your singleness.

Give It Time

Dealing with hurt takes time. I learned to live with the pain, but only by God's grace. After my disappointment with Steve, each day I would get out of bed, my heart aching, my eyes puffed up and red from constant crying. I did not want to get up. How would I deal with this—one more man, one more broken heart? When would the pain leave? Now what? At some point I would have to face family and friends and tell them, "No, Steve didn't work out either." I did not want to talk about it, but I did not have a choice. I just wanted to hide, go away, and hope that this was a very bad dream. Unfortunately, it was my life. How long would I carry this pain?

It was a cold, rainy Saturday morning, and I had slept until about 10:00 A.M. I thought, *Why get up? I think I will just stay in bed and continue to feel sorry for myself,* and that I did. I lay there for a while, but then God reminded me that my negative thinking would only open the door for Satan to flood my mind with continual lies. I knew that I had better change the way I was thinking.

I slowly rolled out of bed and found the book *Heaven: Your Real Home,* by Joni Eareckson Tada. She has ministered to me through the years, but at this time in my life, her words made a significant impact.

I had the pleasure of producing a video and television program with Joni and Kay Arthur called *When the Pain Won't Go Away.* In the video, Joni told her testimony. As a young, vibrant teenage girl, Joni had a diving accident, broke her neck, and became paralyzed from the neck down. She told of friends coming to see her in the hospital, and how they placed a Bible under her bed. As she lay facedown on a Stryker frame, she had to turn the pages of the Bible with a stick placed in her mouth. Joni said she knew her life was going to have to be a choice, "Was I going to be bitter or better?" She said that holding on to God's Word was her strength and that God really does work all things out for our good, even if it meant being in a wheelchair the rest of her life (Romans 8:28).

In *Heaven: Your Real Home*, Joni writes,

> I cannot tell you how much sorrow I've held at bay over the years. Tears could come easily if I allowed myself to think of all the pleasures of movement and sensation I've missed. Diving into a pool and feeling my arms and legs slice through the water. Plucking guitar strings with my fingers. Jogging till my muscles burn. Cracking steam-broiled Maryland crabs with a mallet. Throwing back the covers in the morning and hopping out of bed.[1]

Her words pierced my heart. I felt as though God was clearly speaking to me about not wasting any more time feeling sorry for myself, but to throw back my covers and hop out of bed! I was to continue to live a life that I had lived for years, and that life was through Him. I could find no joy in myself, in my broken dreams, but only in Jesus Christ. And I, too, had a choice. Was I going to be bitter or better?

Revelation gives us a wonderful description of heaven:

And I heard a loud voice from the throne, saying, "Behold, the tabernacle of God is among men, and He will dwell among them, and they shall be His people, and God Himself will be among them, and He will wipe away every tear from their eyes; and there will no longer be any death; there will no longer be any mourning, or crying, or pain; the first things have passed away." And He who sits on the throne said, "Behold, I am making all things new." And He said, "Write, for these words are faithful and true." (Revelation 21:3–5)

These verses comforted me as I focused on what is true—what I know will come to pass. I was reminded that God wants me to realize that this world is not my home. I am here only temporarily while waiting to be with Him permanently in heaven. Do you believe that heaven is real? That it is eternal, that it is your home? Heaven gives us hope beyond this life! Are you like I was . . . looking for everything to be perfect here on earth?

My prayer has become that my circumstances would be for the greater progress of the Gospel. I trust that by remaining single, I am able to encourage others who are single; that they, too, will be willing to wait upon the Lord, knowing that Christ has a perfect plan for their lives. I have chosen to be better, not bitter.

I daily had to hang on to His Word.

Therefore, since we have so great a cloud of witnesses surrounding us, let us also lay aside every encumbrance and the sin which so easily entangles us, and let us run with endurance the race that is set before us, fixing our eyes on Jesus, the author and perfecter of faith, who for the joy set before Him endured the cross, despising the shame, and has sat down at the right hand of the throne of God. For consider Him who has endured such hostility by sinners against Himself, so that you will not grow weary and lose heart. (Hebrews 12:1–3)

Fix Your Eyes on Jesus

Sometimes we look at other people's lives and envy begins to enter into our thoughts. We begin to daydream and wonder, *What if I just had their life?* But as we compare our lives to others, we may be looking at a picture of something that is not real. We live a life of "if only," and life begins to ensnare us with dreams of something that we may see only in the movies.

In the spring of 1912, crowds of people made their way to the edge of the ocean port to see one of the greatest ocean luxury liners ever built, the *Titanic.* The 1997 movie *Titanic* was a huge success, winning eleven Oscars at the Academy Awards, including best picture. This blockbuster was then the most expensive film ever made, costing filmmakers $200 million. What is it about this story that so captivates us?

Do you ever wonder what it would have been like to watch as the great ship started its engines and began to leave the shore of Southampton, expecting to arrive in New York City in record-breaking time? The majority of the well-known passengers on the *Titanic* were American.

Among them were millionaires J. J. Astor and Benjamin Guggenheim. Astor was one of the richest men in the world. Would you have stood there looking with envy, wishing you were one of those people boarding this magnificent ocean liner? Passengers were dressed in their finest custom-tailored clothes, walking toward this grand vessel, and looking with anticipation at the days ahead.

Your imagination begins to run wild, and you start to compare your life to those who seemingly had it all. Before you know it, you're telling yourself what a lousy life you have, and you wonder why you can't go on such a wonderful voyage!

But then, tragedy struck. It was unbelievable. The world was in shock . . .

"On April 15, The New York Times was able to soberly report: New Liner Titanic Hits An Iceberg, Sinking By The Bow At Midnight; Women Put Off In Lifeboats; Last Wireless At 12:27A.M. Blurred."[2] Of the 2,224 people aboard the Titanic, 1,513 died.

Don't you imagine those who decided to be the first to travel on the *Titanic* never considered the fact that it could ever sink? I feel quite sure that those who had wished they could experience such an awesome voyage were extremely grateful they didn't go. If we could only trust our heavenly Father and realize He knows what lies ahead, that He knows what is best for our lives! Certainly, when the disappointments in life come, it's not always easy to see past our hurt and pain. God's Word says, "'For My thoughts are not your thoughts, nor are your ways My ways,' declares the Lord. 'For as the heavens are higher than the earth, so are My ways higher than your ways and My thoughts than your thoughts'" (Isaiah 55:8–9).

Where are you looking? Whose life do you wish you had? On what are you focused? Sometimes the things we think we would love to have, God knows would only destroy us.

You may be reading this book because you can relate to the fact that your prince has not come. The pain of your loneliness is about to kill you. You are tired of being alone.

You may be waiting to get married, waiting to make your first million, waiting to get out of debt, waiting to purchase the next car, waiting to finish school, waiting to go back to school, waiting to get the perfect job, waiting for retirement, waiting for the next vacation.

Or, you may have tried marriage, and it did not work out. You may be waiting on the divorce, waiting for the babies to be out of diapers, waiting for the teenagers to move out of the house.

You may have a strong desire to have children, but at this time in your life you're still single. Possibly due to health reasons you will never have children. For most women it's a natural desire to want children, and this longing doesn't wait quietly until marriage before it's felt.

Waiting . . . waiting . . . waiting . . .

The list could go on and on, but when will your circumstances ever be perfect? And what if that time never comes? When are you going to start living and stop waiting?

Since women are relational, it is normal for us to base our happiness on our relationships. What is normal and what the Lord can do in and through our lives are entirely different issues. If we live our lives depending on someone else to make us happy, our lives will remain like a rollercoaster, only to end up crashing at some point.

Are you simply waiting to find the perfect mate, believing that then you will be happy? What if you could truly be happy, despite your circumstances?

The apostle Paul wrote, from a dark, damp prison cell, about having joy: "Now I want you to know, brethren, that my circumstances have turned out for the greater progress of the gospel, so that my imprisonment in the cause of Christ has become well known throughout the whole praetorian guard and to everyone else" (Philippians 1:12–13).

Paul's passion was touching others with the Gospel, and his happiness was not dependent on his circumstances. His focus was on the Lord—not being in a prison cell. Paul is the perfect example of a life that remains single-minded, despite the enormous challenges he faced in life.

My friend, are you bitter? Are you emotionally exhausted with your hopes of ever finding a mate? Could it be there is bitterness in your life that has been buried so deep you don't even realize it? How's your language? Do you seem to be frustrated all the time? Do the little inconveniences of life really get to you?

Waiting in long lines, traffic, your boss, they all make you angry. If you would be honest with yourself, you're mad, and you may have been for a very long time. Maybe the men in your life have left you scarred and you don't know whom you can trust anymore. With all the hurt you find yourself bitter, but you don't really know how to deal with it.

Bitterness is like a cancer that will grow and eat away at you if not dealt with properly; it will destroy any possibility of joy in your life. Has someone hurt you so deeply that you don't know how you will ever forgive him? The pain has grown deep, but you keep going because that's life. You have to pay the bills.

Do you believe God knows and cares about all of your pain? His Word tells us:

> Let no unwholesome word proceed from your mouth, but only such a word as is good for edification according to the need of the moment, so that it will give grace to those who hear. Do not grieve the Holy Spirit of God, by whom you were sealed for the day of redemption. Let all bitterness and wrath and anger and clamor and slander be put away from you, along with all malice. Be kind to one another, tender-hearted, forgiving each other, just as God in Christ also has forgiven you. (Ephesians 4:29–32)

I love these verses. Notice that as Paul mentions bitterness, he also includes the words *wrath* and *anger*. Bitterness brings out the very worst attributes in a person. But also note the contrast that Paul gives: "Be kind to one another, tender-hearted." Do you desire kindness and tenderness in your life? Can you think of a person you know who has great kindness and tenderness? I have a friend who is probably one of the nicest people I have ever known. Many people love and admire her. Why? She exudes kindness and tenderness. If bitterness is in your life, it's very hard to be this kind of person.

Do you want to be bitter, or do you choose to be better? Often in life we cannot act on what we feel, but what we know. Refuse to let the person who has hurt you take any more of your life! He may have robbed you of plenty of your past, but don't let him take your future.

How do you get past the hurt, the pain, from broken relationships? Run to the living and true God who has forgiven you and who will help you forgive those who have hurt you. He knows all that has happened to you. He cares, He understands. Keep giving it back to Him. You cannot carry this alone, and if you try, the bitterness will destroy you.

Life consists of constant forgiveness. It may be in the daily simple misunderstandings with family or friends, or it could be from enormous heartbreak that has occurred in your life from people who have made very wrong choices that have hurt you deeply.

Your parents may have hurt you. You may have a close friend who has walked away. You may have an ex-husband, a boyfriend, or a fiancé who has chosen someone else over you.

Whoever it was, whenever it was, you must forgive the person and move on. Have you dealt with the hurt from some very old and painful events of your past? Don't stuff it, hide it, bury it, cover it; but deal with it. Give it time. Generally true forgiveness is a process; it will not happen overnight.

You forgive, and forgive, and forgive and, when you

don't feel like it, you forgive again. Jesus tells us this so clearly in His Word. "Then Peter came and said to Him, 'Lord, how often shall my brother sin against me and I forgive him? Up to seven times?' Jesus said to him, 'I do not say to you, up to seven times, but up to seventy times seven'" (Matthew 18:21–22).

We all desire to be whole, free from any bitterness. With complete forgiveness in our hearts, true wholeness is possible. Let go, and let God heal the wounds of all those who have hurt you. Can you sing, "It is well with my soul"?

I love this amazing song that was penned by a man who had unbelievable heartbreak in his life. Horatio G. Spafford wrote the words of this song after losing all of his children in a tragic accident. The *Ville du Havre* collided with an English sailing ship, the *Loch Earn*. Daughters— Maggie, Tanetta, Annie, and Bessie—were killed. Spafford chose to be better, not bitter.

IT IS WELL WITH MY SOUL

When peace, like a river, attendeth my way,
When sorrows like sea billows roll;
Whatever my lot, Thou hast taught me to say,
"It is well, it is well, with my soul."

Though Satan should buffet, though trials should come,
Let this blest assurance control,
That Christ has regarded my helpless estate,
And hath shed His own blood for my soul.

My sin—oh, the bliss of this glorious thought—
My sin—not in part, but the whole—
Is nailed to the cross, and I bear it no more,
Praise the Lord, praise the Lord, O my soul!

And, Lord, haste the day when the faith shall be sight,
The clouds be rolled back as a scroll,
The trump shall resound, and the Lord shall descend,
"Even so"—it is well with my soul.

It is well with my soul,
It is well, it is well with my soul.
                              —Horatio G. Spafford, 1873
                              music by Philip P. Bliss, 1876

NOTES

1. Joni Eareckson Tada, *Heaven: Your Real Home* (Grand Rapids: Zondervan, 1995), 29.
2. Richard Howells, *The Myth of the Titanic* (New York: St. Martin's Press, 1999), 27.

Did Your
Prince Leave?

Everyone has a story. I would love to be able to sit down with you over a great cup of coffee and hear yours. For many, life has been hard. All too often our pasts can overtake us. If not handled correctly, they can destroy our future.

Maybe you have gone through a divorce, you're a single mom, or your husband died much sooner than you ever dreamed he would. I have three wonderful friends who, despite the heartbreak, the pain, the magnitude of their hurt, have chosen God to be their source of joy and strength. They truly understand that it's not how you start in life that matters; it's how you finish.

Christie's Story

Have you ever thought about life simply being a series of choices we make every day? Christie's life was a progression of choices. But never was it Christie's desire or her choice to be divorced. Can you relate?

The vows said on her wedding day were words her husband had not kept. With all her heart she had meant "till death do us part," but later the words she heard were "I want a divorce!" The sting, the enormous heartbreak of these painful words changed her world in a way she never dreamed possible.

Christie was the first of four girls who were raised in a wonderful home with parents who affirmed their children in every way possible. She was encouraged to dream big, love life, and seek God. From a young age, Christie loved to dance. Ballet, jazz, tap, she did it all. She had a real talent, and at age twelve she became a charter member of the local Ballet Theater. She fully planned to spend the rest of her life dancing.

In some ways she thought as Shakespeare, "All the world is a stage . . . " and for Christie it was just the place to be.

With years of dancing, being loved, having approval from family and friends, Christie was happy. The next step would be college. She started out as a ballet major, but she soon realized she needed something else that might be a bit more practical. While working on her BS in journalism and advertising, she met Dave. He charmed Christie by lavishing her with lots of gifts. He would walk in the room . . . and, well, there was just something about his cologne, his demeanor, and his praise that won her heart.

Christie and Dave had a fabulous wedding with eight hundred people in attendance. Christie says that as she walked down the aisle with her dad, the thought entered her mind, *Dave may not be the one.* But she thought, *He will change; we can work through our differences.*

The desire to be married can be so great, and often the obvious warning signs about a person get lost in the whirlwind of "falling in love." As they say, love really can be blind.

After the wedding and playing house a bit, the reality of marriage became very sobering. Day after day Christie began to live in a world she had never known. Why did her husband, whom she thought loved her, continue to verbally abuse her? How could the man, whom she thought was an occasional drinker, in reality be an alcoholic? Living with an alcoholic was unbearable. Why did it seem like nothing Christie did was ever right? After all the years of trying everything she could possibly try to make it work, she still heard the words, "I don't love you anymore." His greatest loves were hunting and fishing. Their marriage was torn apart and over.

After Dave moved out, a great depression that she couldn't shake settled over Christie. She had been rejected and heard the same negative words over and over, and in time she believed them.

Christie told me about the darkest time in her life . . .

It's like a blanket of hopelessness and despair covered me mentally and physically. About two weeks after Dave left, I had a hard time functioning at all. I kept listening to the same tape, the same thing over and over in my mind, every wrong thing I had ever done, every outburst of anger, every hurtful word I had hurled at Dave. Unfortunately, the tape (my thoughts) never played the other side of the story; it only focused on my actions.

Since our house had been burglarized, I started sleeping with a gun under my pillow. What a horrible way I was living! As I continued with my negative thinking, thoughts of worthlessness kept coming into my mind. I wondered if I mattered to anyone. Dave abandoned me because he had grown to hate me. I had told no one I was going through this, so the phone did not ring, and the isolation I was feeling was overwhelming. I know for a fact this is when Satan was working the hardest.

He wanted me to take my life. I sat in the dark and honestly thought, *Why not end it all? This is more than I can take.* But, praise God, He was greater. I had given my life to the Lord at age eighteen, but at this young age, I focused on my life rather than His Word. I had no idea of the importance of reading and studying the Bible. I had not been grounded in the truths to help me stand firm and keep me from all my anger.

In my frustration and anger, I broke every door in the house. The continual battles in my mind, the bitterness, the brokenness had taken over, and I decided it was time to get help. I finally had a breakdown.

All the pain, all the suffering, all the years of misery were worth it. I can honestly tell you that, because it drove me to the true and living God, Jesus Christ. What Satan meant for evil, God meant for good. I got involved in a dynamic church that taught the Word of God. I began attending Bible studies and prayer meetings. I did not change overnight . . . it took time.

Damaged people have so many protective layers around them that have to be peeled back one layer at a time. It's like learning to walk all over again. You take the first step, then the second one. When you get tired, you rest.

Today I am free. I am whole. I know who I am in Christ. I have no more nightmares or thoughts of rejection and abuse. God created me knowing full well the mistakes I would make. His grace and mercy are sufficient no matter what you go through. He has proven Himself faithful to me over and over again. Truly, through it all, I learned my only hope is in the Lord. Like the psalm says, I had to put my complete trust and hope in His Word.

"I wait for the Lord, my soul does wait, and in His word do I hope. My soul waits for the Lord more than the watchmen for the morning; indeed, more than the watchmen for the morning" (Psalm 130:5–6).

When I first met Christie I would never have imagined that she had experienced such extreme rejection and pain. Christie is now vibrant and happy, and she loves to listen to the voice of the Lord and watch and wait for His next great adventure. She is a true example of Christ's supernatural healing in a person's life.

Has someone told you, "I don't love you anymore?" Maybe it was not in a divorce, but you were engaged to be married, or you have been in a long relationship, and the man in your life walked away. No matter the situation, the rejection and the heartbreak of these words continue to stay in your mind, and it is difficult to get past the pain of it all. It's so easy to want a quick fix to your pain, because it hurts too much.

For many the answer is to find someone else as soon as possible. Your cry may be, "Would someone just fill this empty void of being single?" Yes, I believe most single women have felt this, but joy is possible no matter what you have been through. The answer is certainly not to rush into another relationship. Let God heal you first.

Martha's Story

It fascinates me to see marriages today that are able to weather the storms that many marriages undergo. My dear friend Martha has lived such a marriage. After thirty-five years together, certainly two had become one.

Martha married her first love when she was nineteen years old. Excited about marriage and her new life with Bobby, they later experienced the joy of having two wonderful baby boys. The growing together . . . the learning to be a family . . . the issues that daily life brings . . . time seemed to pass quickly. Days turned into months, and months turned into years. They had moved into a wonderful time in their lives.

In many ways, they had grown up together. They had years of learning each other's likes and dislikes. Years of not even having to speak but knowing what the other was thinking. Years of putting up the Christmas tree and doing everything together for the holidays. Years of taking walks together, vacationing together, having meals together. Years of laughing, crying, and sleeping together. Years of simply being together and being comforted with each other's company. At this point, there was not much uncovered —they knew the imperfections, and they still loved each other. Whatever happened, they would be together.

Martha and I sat and talked over dinner, and she began to tell me about the night she got the news . . .

When Bobby got sick it all happened so fast. I will never forget when I got the phone call from friends who said, "They think Bobby has had a stroke." I hung up the phone in a daze, in disbelief. I sat down trying to comprehend it and said to myself, "This is real." All the uncertainties, all the hopes, all the possibilities that Bobby might not be as sick as we thought ended that night.

My friends took me to the hospital, and when we got there, I saw Bobby lying on a stretcher. Seeing him like that was indescribable. What was I going to do? Later that evening I heard the doctor tell me, "Bobby has a brain tumor, and he must be admitted into the hospital." After hearing these words, my life was never the same.

How was I going to cope? How could I deal with knowing, and even facing the reality of the fact that Bobby was going to die? Certainly I knew that God could heal him, but by talking with the doctor I learned that 95 percent of men Bobby's age died if they acquired this type of malignant brain tumor. I was so shocked with what I was being told that I could hardly breathe. I began to cry as I wondered how I was going to tell my grown sons. How was I going to go on? A deep somberness settled over my life, and it didn't go away for a very long time. I could not just fall apart like I felt like doing.

The man who had been my provider, my protector, my love was slowing dying. The sad fact is that I lost Bobby long before he actually died. I watched as his normal thought processes began to leave him. I will never forget when we were coming back from vacation, and Bobby started giving directions for getting us home. It was frightening. He had driven these roads for years, but he was giving totally wrong directions. That was our last vacation together.

It was now time to walk in all the truths I had learned. God used every trial I'd experienced throughout my life to prepare me for this. An army of people came around and filled in the gaps when all I could do was try to keep one foot in front of the other. I took life one day at a time; I could handle no more. I clung to the Word of God. I knew that my life was not my own. I had given my life to Him years ago.

When Bobby died, the pain was excruciating. I was not bitter at God—I knew that God gives life and takes life; it was just much sooner than I could have ever imagined. The life I knew was no more. At times when I thought I could not take it anymore, I would get an encouraging card or a sweet phone call from family and friends. I knew people were praying for me. It made a tremendous difference.

I never realized Bobby did so much. It was hard doing everything—all the shopping, banking, housework, the yard, the car—it was just so much. Emotionally I had to deal with the vacant seat at the family gatherings. It was extremely difficult.

I moved into the singles world kicking and screaming. It was time to face it and begin to walk it out. A couple of weeks after the funeral, I was so tired of hurting. I woke up and the thought came to my mind, *Then don't!* I pictured myself with a smile on my face. I had hurt for so long that it felt wrong. It frightened me to be happy. But I was sick of hurting. I pictured myself smiling again, and I thought, *Just today I will try to smile—just today.* I knew if a negative thought entered my mind, I had to fight it. I knew it would put me in a downward spiral that I could not afford to have. A verse I held on to was "Do not fear, for I am with you; Do not anxiously look about you, for I am your God. I will strengthen you, surely I will help you, surely I will uphold you with My righteous right hand" (Isaiah 41:10).

And that He did. Every day I would get up, knowing that my only strength was in Him. But day after day, I would say, "I will smile today for the glory of God." Somewhere between just making it through each day, trusting, praying, being with friends, going to church, being with family, I realized I was smiling again, and it was not taking a lot of effort. Joy was back in my life and, yes, God had become my husband in ways I never dreamed possible.

I have watched Martha's life as she has learned to be a widow. The Spirit of God is evident in her life. She will tell you that alone it would have been impossible, but with God all things are possible (Mark 10:27).

When tragedy strikes in a person's life, it's as if the person has been in a very bad car accident. A body cast is put on, and it is very hard to live with. But each day the person learns to take baby steps.

Today the cast is gone, and Martha will never walk the same again because she had to find a "new normal" for her life. The realities of all the Scriptures she has ever known are the very bedrock of her existence. She had become one with Bobby just as the Scripture tells us marriage will do, but that one was torn apart when Bobby died. But thank God, He is the healer of all the broken pieces. Martha is excited about all that He is doing in her life. He is opening up doors of ministry she never dreamed possible. Her "new normal" is good, and she is enjoying life and all that God has for her.

Maybe you should find a "new normal" for your life. Is there someone in your life who should not be there? You may not have lost a husband to cancer, but you need to lose the man in your life (assuming you are not married to him). Has he been in your life so long that you cannot imagine life without him? Maybe the normal for you has become an unhealthy relationship.

If you would truly be honest, you know he is bad news. He is not the kind of man you really are looking for, but you're too scared to let him go. Yes, it will feel different for a while, but if you continue in this relationship it could be very destructive to your future. Be obedient to whatever the Lord tells you to do. You will never be sorry.

Cheryl's Story

When Cheryl and John boarded the 747, heading to France for their honeymoon, they had no idea what lay ahead for them in the months and years that followed. Cheryl was only twenty, and she was excited about her future as a new wife. Both Cheryl and John were young and extremely naive about how marriage works. They knew one thing, that they loved each other, and isn't that all that really matters? Both were heavily involved in drugs and alcohol. Life was one big party. For a while, the passion, the parties, and a life full of possibilities for a future together seemed to keep them happy.

After five years of marriage, Cheryl became pregnant and gave birth to a beautiful baby girl. Things changed as Cheryl began to question what life really was all about. She knew something was missing. Having a baby had not been the answer to the growing discontentment. Trying to talk with John only made matters worse. He seemed to have no idea what Cheryl was feeling. There was no communication, no oneness, no true intimacy.

Almost three years later, their second child was born. Cheryl had a home with two children and a husband, but she had never felt so alone. She had come to the very end—she decided that the pain of this life was too much. One unforgettable night, Cheryl stood staring into her bathroom mirror with a razor blade in hand and thought, *I cannot take it anymore.* The battle to take her life raged in her mind. But instead, she cried out to the Lord, and the Spirit of God came upon Cheryl unlike anything she had ever known—His presence powerfully moved upon her. She fell to the floor and told God to take her life. Take all the pain, the hurt, the loneliness, the fear, the rejection, but most of all take whatever He could do with her life and use it.

True joy moved into her life, but the conflicts and misunderstandings with John grew even greater. Cheryl was completely different. John thought Cheryl was on some new religious kick and it would pass. But it was very real, and Cheryl lived on faith and hope that this marriage could work. Unfortunately, John continued looking for everything in this life to bring him happiness—drugs, alcohol, and later, other women.

Cheryl was devastated. What now? Six years after their third child was born, John moved out of the house, only to come back ten days later. The emotional drain on Cheryl was overwhelming. It was only her faith and strong prayer life that carried her through. Psalm 119:50 says, "This is my comfort in my affliction, that Your word has revived me." And it had revived and sustained Cheryl. Eighteen years of marriage, three children, and another family broken. The only answer for John was to finally leave, and this time it was for good.

When I first met Cheryl and heard her story, I wanted to know how she did it. She was a single mom, working, and doing all she knew to raise three children on a very limited income.

My divorce papers were served to me the day before my fortieth birthday. I thought, *What a present!* Here I was, forty years old, divorced, with three children. They were nine, twelve, and fourteen. I had no job, and had not worked in over fifteen years. Who in the world would hire me? I felt the Lord impressed upon me to go back to school. In many ways this did not seem logical. Who would pay the bills? How would I pay for school? I felt strongly that I was to do this, when many thought I was crazy.

What a great surprise it was when my father paid my way to school and thought it was a wonderful idea! I had no money coming in regularly. One thing I did early with my children was to teach them to trust God to provide. I would gather the kids together and we would pray. There were times we had little to no money. I will never forget the day when I got a check in the mail for four hundred dollars and a note that said, "No good thing does He withhold from those who walk uprightly" (Psalm 84:11). Over and over we prayed, we waited, and God took care of us.

Very early I began to see that the Lord Jesus Christ was my husband, and He would provide all that we needed. "For your husband is your Maker, whose name is the Lord of hosts" (Isaiah 54:5). These words became reality for me, not just meaningless words on paper. I lived in the truth of these verses.

I love being a mother. I love to cook. But the pressure mounted. I could not do it all. I couldn't, but God reminded me, "You're right, but I can." Only in His strength is it possible to have a true family life, one that can really be full of joy despite the enormous stress. After looking back in some of my journals, I found where I had written, "I am trying not to be anxious. My creed to live by this school year will be, *'I can do all things through Him who strengthens me'* (Philippians 4:13)." Daily He gave me the strength to keep going, to keep growing, to keep knowing that His love truly is sufficient.

After finishing school, I earnestly cried out to God, "Where do you want me to work?" After a few weeks, the phone rang and it was the director of a small, nonprofit Christian organization. I had a job interview and I was offered the job. Nothing could have been better for me. It was the perfect fit. I am still employed there ten years later.

Certainly in the early days of the divorce my emotions were full of rage, rejection, fear, anguish, and sadness. The kids and I would sit on the bed holding each other. We would cry and sing "Jesus Loves Me." This is all we knew. Through many trials and lots of difficult days, God was stretching and molding me. Daily, it came down to this— did I trust Him or not?

There were days I did not feel like I could go on. I would come home from work exhausted. I wanted to fall into bed, but I couldn't. There was dinner to cook, homework to get done, and clothes to wash, not to mention trying to keep the house cleaned up and in order!

When we first told the children we were divorcing, the two older children screamed "No!" at the top of their lungs. The youngest one just cried silently; he seemed to stuff his pain. My oldest son was filled with anger. I would get phone calls at work and it would sound like World War III breaking out. My daughter was getting more rebellious. Sometimes the fear that I would totally lose control overwhelmed me. I prayed constantly. I refused to believe all the statistics I heard about kids growing up in single-parent homes. Instead, I believed in the keeping power of God and prayer.

What a joy it is to see what God has done in Cheryl's life and with her children. This past year, her youngest son left for college. Her daughter has graduated cum laude from the College of Charleston and is currently working with learning-disabled children. Her oldest son is a senior in college and will graduate with a degree in conservational biology. All have given their hearts to the Lord and know that He is able to see them through life's most difficult circumstances.

Yes, it was in the unexpected miracles of everyday life that the Lord took her hand and said, "Cheryl, just today, trust Me. Can you do that?" and Cheryl said, "Yes."

Today, are you saying yes to the Lord who knows your pain? You may be a single mom, and you're overwhelmed with the task before you. You simply cannot see how you will ever be happy again. Life seems to be one big complicated mess.

Christie, Martha, and Cheryl would all love to give you a hug and tell you they understand, and truly they do. Maybe you have gone through some of the exact same heartaches. A broken family, a husband's death, or you simply cannot stand the loneliness that you feel. Your pain is real, but don't let it overtake you; don't let it get the best of you. Often we think if we had not made such wrong choices, everything would be different. Yes, we suffer consequences from not seeking God about the decisions we make. However, whatever you have been through, God will use you if will let Him.

What is your story? Maybe you haven't experienced a divorce, but you understand the heartbreak of a man walking out of your life. Pain is pain, and whatever you have been through, it hurts deeply.

It's important that we learn from each other. If the Lord can bring Christie, Martha, and Cheryl through all their pain, He can do the same for you. Seek Him, serve Him, surrender all that you have, all that has you, and let Him be your true strength, your true joy.

True Joy

Would you consider yourself a joyful person? What makes you happy? Are you content? Contentment is one of life's greatest attributes. Where does it come from? Are you dependent on a man in your life to give you happiness? For many years I was.

As a young girl, I was a vibrant, happy child with a heart that was extremely naive as I became emotionally smitten with boys. No one taught me this; no one told me to like boys, I just did. So who would have thought that this boy-crazy little girl would grow up and still never marry? It wasn't because I didn't have wonderful parents and good role models to follow.

My mother went to a lot of trouble getting four kids dressed and ready for church. We all thought it might be a good idea to show up for Sunday school and church since my father was the pastor. Church suppers, children's choir practice, and vacation Bible school were all a part of my childhood. How very blessed I am to have this kind of heritage. But, like everyone else, I still had choices to make as I began growing up and my parents started letting go.

How does a young girl question what her father tells a congregation of people? The idea that the Bible could be false never entered my mind. I was in church most Sundays; this was our life. I believed in God, but I still wasn't a Christian.

God's Word says, "You believe that God is one. You do well; the demons also believe, and shudder" (James 2:19). I needed more than just an intellectual belief. I was far from a surrendered life to the Lord. I believe Satan is happy to have people in church who think they are saved, but who aren't.

I understand this so clearly, because even being a pastor's daughter, I was certainly deceived. The boyfriends in my life got the majority of my attention. My obsession with boys hurt my grades, hindered my time with my family, and most certainly impeded any kind of walk with the Lord.

The 1970s was a time when the hippie movement was on the rise, and the thinking that Christianity was a way to live was being challenged by Hollywood and many of our entertainers. The top love songs flooded my mind at a very young age. The Beatles were the craze. I sang "I Want to Hold Your Hand" over and over. Two of my favorite movies were *Romeo and Juliet* and *Love Story*. My mind was inundated with the world's thinking, and I had no idea what was happening to me.

I don't believe a person can continue to fill his mind with wrong thinking and not begin to live it out at some point. You have probably heard the phrase "garbage in = garbage out." How true this is. The Bible clearly says, "For as he thinks within himself, so he is" (Proverbs 23:7). Not all the songs and movies I liked were "garbage," but I didn't have enough of God's Word in my life to give me a proper perspective.

Even with all these outside influences bombarding my mind, I was a pretty self-righteous young girl. When I was about ten years old, I remember telling my older brothers and sister that I would *never* drink or smoke! I don't know if I thought those were two of the worst things a person could do, but I remember feeling pretty passionate about this. Those pious words quickly changed as I began to be tempted with the partying scene that most of my high school friends were beginning to experience.

I had finally reached the time that I had been waiting for, my first real date. My boyfriend was tall, blond, and handsome. I thought I had found true love. After a few Friday-night dates, he began pressuring me to drink. At first it made me angry, but after a while it didn't seem so bad. Unfortunately, I later gave in to the temptation.

I never realized that this one drink would open the door to more and more alcohol and that it would take me away from God and into a world of great peer pressure. Weekend parties became a normal way of life. The sad thing about this was that the majority of my high school friends attended these parties. Where were the Christians? We thought *we* were the Christians! Many of us were out late on Saturday night, but we were in church the next morning. It still never entered my mind that I was lost and headed for hell.

Even if I had kept my list of "dos and don'ts," it still would not have saved me from eternal destruction. No, the problem was my lack of faith—I had no relationship with Jesus Christ, who would have guided me through those years. The Bible says, "For by grace you have been saved through faith; and that not of yourselves, it is the gift of God; not as a result of works, so that no one may boast. For we are His workmanship, created in Christ Jesus for good works, which God prepared beforehand so that we would walk in them" (Ephesians 2:8–10). I had a lot of growing to do before I understood this truth.

Fall was in the air, classes were in session, and my life seemed full. It was my sophomore year of college, and I loved all that the academic world had to offer. My biggest challenge—studying. I looked for every extracurricular activity I could find. I was on the women's tennis team, sang in the college choir, and was in a small singing ensemble.

I will never forget when I was asked if I wanted to be in the school's beauty pageant. I thought, "Why not?" Another good excuse not to study! One deciding factor about this contest, there was no swimsuit competition! The night of the pageant each contestant began by walking to the microphone, giving her name, and telling something interesting about herself. I remember saying, "Hello! I am Kathleen Hardaway. 'The Lord is my light and my salvation; whom shall I fear? The Lord is the strength of my life; of whom shall I be afraid?'" (Psalm 27:1 KJV).

As I reflect back to that night, in many ways I had no idea what I was saying. Yes, I thought I believed this truth, but I had never really walked in the realities of it. Up until this point in my life, I didn't have many dark days. I certainly wasn't afraid of much, and I was walking in my strength and not the Lord's. But things changed.

True Conversion

I began to examine the way I was living. I started to question my drinking and partying. I struggled with thinking that this was not the way I should live. My Bible study consisted of trying to open a daily devotion in hopes that God would speak to me. Even in those few devotions that I occasionally read, God did speak to me and began to draw me to Himself. "Draw near to God and He will draw near to you" (James 4:8) became reality to me.

All the partying really bothered me, and the pull that this had over me upset me greatly. I would decide that I would not go out and drink anymore, but within just a few short weeks, I would be out doing the same things. I began to worry because it did not matter how hard I tried, I couldn't stop. I thought, *What is wrong with me?*

The book of Romans tells us, "Do you not know that when you present yourselves to someone as slaves for obedience, you are slaves of the one whom you obey, either of sin resulting in death, or of obedience resulting in righteousness?" (Romans 6:16). I had become enslaved to this lifestyle and did not know that I needed to be set free.

I didn't realize it then, but all the truths I had learned

at an early age had made a significant impact in my life. When I was a freshman in college, I received a note from my father, postmarked February 12, 1976. Dad's closing comments read:

> I am proud of you in so many ways, and I have turned all four of you (children) over to the Lord, for guidance, deliverance, help and love. Always remember Jesus through the Holy Spirit is sufficient to handle all problems, especially boy-girl-girl-boy ones. I count on Him for help all the time. Keep going on His daily bread.
>
> Love and Kisses, Dad

I have kept his letter, and it is still applicable to my life today. What powerful words my father had prayed for me. He seemed to be keenly aware of the fact that his daughter stayed on this "boy crazy" track, and it did not look like I was going to change anytime in the near future. He had already seen much of the heartache I had experienced, and he knew it seemed to be an unending trial for me.

In 1979, during my senior year in college, I attended a Billy Graham crusade in Nashville, where I grew up. As I sat and listened to this great man of God, I was enormously challenged. I had to come to terms with the direction I wanted my life to go. There were questions that I had to answer. Had I given everything to Him? Did I love Him with all my heart, soul, and mind? Did I want to live my life completely for Him? I knew I needed to give it all to Him and stop living a double standard. That night, when the invitation to receive Jesus Christ was given, I went down front and prayed. This was the beginning of a major turning point in my life.

From College to the Workplace

After graduating from college, I was determined to find a teaching job that I had worked so long and hard to attain. Résumés were sent, job applications were filled out, but there were no offers. The fall school semester started, and I realized that my goal of teaching school was not going to happen. In many ways my world was shattered.

For most of my life up until that point, if I worked for something, I usually got results. Why did I work so relentlessly to get a degree, and it seemed to get me nowhere? God had a much better plan for my life, but all I could think of was, I had no idea what I was going to do.

Has your world fallen apart, and you don't know what to do? Maybe you're at a crossroads, and you don't have a clue what's going to happen next. Whatever has happened in your life, can you consider that it could be for your good? This is a difficult thing to think, when the circumstances look so bad. When I look back over some of the major disappointments in my life, they were the very best things that could have happened to me. God had finally gotten my attention. Could it be He is trying to get yours?

If I had only known God's Word that says, "'For My thoughts are not your thoughts, nor are your ways My ways,' declares the Lord. 'For as the heavens are higher than the earth, so are My ways higher than your ways and My thoughts than your thoughts'" (Isaiah 55:8–9).

My dreams were high, but those feelings had crashed. I fell into a great depression, so unlike me. I had always been full of life and could quickly get over just about anything. This time it was very different—I was mad at the world.

I will never forget my sister asking me, "Don't you have faith?" Her comment rang in my ear. "Do you not trust Him?" I had come to a major turning point in my life. Did I completely trust God in circumstances I did not like? My sister was right. Where was my faith?

I had been so depressed that I grew tired of being down, so I finally looked up. I prayed a simple prayer. I said, "God, I don't really understand why You don't want me to teach school, but I trust You. Lord, whatever You have for my life, I want to live for You, no matter what it is. The drinking, the boyfriends—take everything in my life that is not pleasing to You. I don't want to live my way any longer."

I believe it was at this point that I was truly born again. I finally understood what true salvation meant. The Lord led me to a great Bible-teaching church, and I began to hunger after His Word. Going to church and learning the truths from the Bible changed my life.

Freedom

I was totally set free from alcohol. It did not happen overnight; I had to constantly die to this habit. Over and over, I gave it back to the Lord, saying, "I can't, but You can help me through this," and within a few months my drinking days were over.

I determined that all I did from that point on would be to live a life that honored and glorified the Lord. I also had decided to date only godly men. The joy that filled my heart was so real that I was no longer dependent on a man's attention or a relationship in order to be happy. Jesus Christ had come to live in my life, and this new life gave me more happiness than I had ever known.

I loved going to church. The praise and worship were unlike anything I had ever known. It was not a worked up, emotional kind of experience, but there was freedom in the worship. The Spirit of the Lord was ever present in those services. The pastor seemed to teach just the words I needed to hear, and it was straight from God's Word, the Bible. I had never felt this much joy in my entire life! Nothing from my past matched this changed life that I received through Jesus Christ.

"Therefore if anyone is in Christ, he is a new creature; the old things passed away; behold, new things have come" (2 Corinthians 5:17). I was, in fact, a completely different person. This verse described *me!*

I truly believe that there is no higher calling in life than to serve the Lord and walk in true obedience to Him. My career plans, goals, and dreams did not compare to giving my life to Jesus Christ. There is no greater joy than to be in His presence . . . in honor of and admiration for all that He has done.

"You will make known to me the path of life; in Your presence is fullness of joy; in Your right hand there are

pleasures forever" (Psalm 16:11). This is one of my favorite verses in the entire Bible. I finally understood what
true joy really means—walking in His presence, being
completely surrendered and obedient to Him.

I trust that you have given your life to the Lord Jesus,
but if not, aren't you tired of doing it your way? Are you
miserable, worn out, sick of life? Maybe your husband has
left you. Maybe your kids are driving you crazy and you're
tired of trying to raise them alone. Maybe you cannot believe you're still single. Maybe your boyfriend just decided
to leave you and date someone else. Has life become one
big disappointment? I understand.

There is an answer to all the confusion, heartache, and
disappointments in life. Jesus said, "I came that they may
have life, and have it abundantly" (John 10:10b).

Jesus came knowing that nothing we could ever do
would put us in right standing with God. He "died for our
sins according to the Scriptures, and that He was buried,
and that He was raised on the third day according to the
Scriptures, and that He appeared to Cephas, then to the
twelve. After that He appeared to more than five hundred
brethren at one time . . . then He appeared to James, then
to all the apostles" (1 Corinthians 15:3b–7).

Prior to this, the only way sins were forgiven was
through sacrifices that were made in the tabernacle and
later in the temple, pointing ahead to Christ's final sacrifice. Enormous effort was made for everything to be sacri-
ficed just as the old covenant instructed. But, praise God,
Jesus was our sacrifice. He paid it all, once and for all!

But when Christ appeared as a high priest of the good things to come, He entered through the greater and more perfect tabernacle, not made with hands, that is to say, not of this creation; and not through the blood of goats and calves, but through His own blood, He entered the holy place once for all, having obtained eternal redemption. For if the blood of goats and bulls and the ashes of a heifer sprinkling those who have been defiled sanctify for the cleansing of the flesh, how much more will the blood of Christ, who through the eternal Spirit offered Himself without blemish to God, cleanse your conscience from dead works to serve the living God? For this reason He is the mediator of a new covenant, so that, since a death has taken place for the redemption of the transgressions that were committed under the first covenant, those who have been called may receive the promise of the eternal inheritance. (Hebrews 9:11–15)

The price was paid through Jesus, the true and living God. Jesus, born of a virgin, chose to die for me. The apostle Paul wrote:

But if there is no resurrection of the dead, not even Christ has been raised; and if Christ has not been raised, then our preaching is vain, your faith also is vain. Moreover we are even found to be false witnesses of God, because we testified against God that He raised Christ, whom He did not raise, if in fact the dead are not raised. (1 Corinthians 15:13–15)

I love these verses. If there had been no resurrection, Paul's preaching was in vain. If Christ was not raised from the dead, our faith is in vain. This is the very essence of the Christian faith. Either Christ is the Son of God or He isn't. Jesus said, "I am the way, and the truth, and the life; no one comes to the Father but through Me" (John 14:6). Do you believe this verse? If it is true, then all the arguments for other religions cannot be true. Jesus' death, burial, and resurrection were the very turning point in all of history. *The world has never been the same.*

Have you ever thought about that? We now have B.C., before Christ was born, and A.D. (Latin *anno Domini*), since Christ was born. The church age had begun, and over two thousand years later, it continues.

Is this a fairy tale or a fable? Was Jesus a liar? Was He simply a good teacher, or is He the Son of God? Is this just another religion, like countless others? Who really knows the truth? What is truth anyway? These are all questions that I certainly pray you have taken seriously and have sought to understand and answer.

Maybe you have heard the gospel all your life. You, too, were brought up in the church. Sometimes I think those who have grown up in church are so familiar with the Scriptures that they never really think about what they mean. Satan loves for us to have an intellectual knowledge about Jesus that stays in our heads and never moves to our hearts.

That is where I was, believing all the Scriptures, but never truly repenting, never truly trusting that God is sufficient to meet my every need . . . never truly asking the Lord what He wanted for my life.

The Lord says, "Take up your cross and follow Me."

If anyone wishes to come after Me, he must deny himself, and take up his cross and follow Me. For whoever wishes to save his life will lose it, but whoever loses his life for My sake and the gospel's will save it. For what does it profit a man to gain the whole world, and forfeit his soul? For what will a man give in exchange for his soul? (Mark 8:34–37)

So often we want Christianity on our terms . . . our way . . . holding on to the sins in life that we believe aren't so bad. It is frightening to think where I would be if I had not finally surrendered everything—my all, my life—to Him. But through His love and mercy, He drew me in His time and in His way. I am forever grateful.

Is It About Sex or Is It About Love?

"I just want someone to love me." Unfortunately, somewhere in this strong desire to be loved, lust may confuse your feelings—and at times it may be hard to tell the difference between the two. All too often the quest for love is found in all the wrong places.

Is it difficult for you to live a pure and righteous life? In today's world, it's important that you stand stronger than ever before, because the temptations that we face are great.

We live in one of the most sex-crazed, lustful periods in history. Certainly during the Greek empire and other historical periods, sexual immorality had its driving forces in culture. Immorality has been a problem with every society, but today it may be greater than at any other time in history.

The technological age has brought immorality into

our living rooms through television, the Internet, VCRs, DVD players, and even through our phone lines. Now with the click of a mouse, the vilest, most perverted acts can be seen on countless numbers of Websites on the Internet. "Playboy has its own web-site with over 18,000 subscribers and an average of 4.7 million hits in one seven-day period."[1] Over four million hits in one week, and this is just one site!

To find pornography, a person used to have to go to a back-alley, X-rated adult bookstore. Now it can come instantly into a home or office through a computer—unsolicited. What has happened to America and our world? These are issues that we're up against as we attempt to live a holy life.

We have had vast numbers of warnings concerning the dangers of pornography and premarital sex, but our culture continues to turn its back on the absolute truths of God's Word. Because of our compromises, we have made our own Sodom and Gomorrah. It's now difficult even to walk through a checkout aisle at the grocery store without seeing sensual images on almost every magazine cover. Immorality and pornography have become one of the greatest problems our country faces. We have opened "Pandora's box," and there appears to be no way of shutting it.

In the days of Sodom and Gomorrah, immorality flooded the land and its people, so much so that God chose to destroy these cities. "And the Lord said, 'The outcry of Sodom and Gomorrah is indeed great, and their sin is exceedingly grave.' . . . Then the Lord rained on Sodom and Gomorrah brimstone and fire from the Lord out of heaven, and He overthrew those cities, and all the valley, and all the inhabitants of the cities, and what grew on the ground" (Genesis 18:20; 19:24–25).

It is clearly seen throughout Scripture that God takes immorality and sex outside of marriage very seriously. Over and over again the Bible states that there will be serious consequences to sexual activity outside the parameters God has set for us. "For this is the will of God, your sanctification; that is, that you abstain from sexual immorality" (1 Thessalonians 4:3).

A Holy Lifestyle

The Bible gives us no other choice than to remain pure in our singleness. "It is written, 'You shall be holy, for I am holy'" (1 Peter 1:16). If you do not have a passion to be holy, then trying to live a pure lifestyle will be close to impossible. In the Sermon on the Mount, Jesus teaches, "Blessed are those who hunger and thirst for righteousness, for they shall be satisfied" (Matthew 5:6).

So many are looking to find some kind of satisfaction in their sexual pleasures outside of marriage, but Jesus says it is in our righteousness that we will be satisfied. "Blessed are the pure in heart, for they shall see God" (Matthew 5:8). Do you desire purity in your life? Really desire it? Do you care more about pleasing God than yourself? This *must* be your motivation for purity.

A holy and righteous life is not a chore of living under a list of dos and don'ts. It will be a passion in you to desire purity above your emotions and what feels good. But re-member, it will go against what the world is doing. *Purity* and *chastity* are words not often used in our culture's best-selling love songs, magazines, books, movies, or, sadly, not even in some churches.

I have heard countless stories of the devastating effects promiscuity has had on the lives of people simply because they chose to live outside God's precepts. Marriages have fallen apart. Young girls have gotten pregnant. Women and men have turned to same-sex partners. Pornography has engulfed and ensnared lives, and incest has destroyed families. And sadly, the AIDS virus still kills thousands. Even with all of this hurt and pain, people continue to live their way instead of God's.

Today's Culture

It breaks my heart to see the overwhelming changes that have taken place in our country concerning sex. Our teenagers are inundated with pop stars who seem to sell their very souls in order to reach the masses. Having a good voice is not necessarily a prerequisite for becoming a talent in today's generation, but looking and being sexy is a must! As the stars perform, the dances are sensual, and their wardrobe leaves them only half dressed. The lyrics are often an abomination to God.

Our culture appears to have chosen many lifestyles completely different from the way God intended. Sex be-fore marriage, couples living together, same-sex partners, you name it, anything goes. Although it appears that the norm has changed, does this make it right? It has become evident that our society left its sexual morals a very long time ago, and today's youth are suffering greatly because of it.

I wish I could tell you that I have had a perfect past, but I have kissed a lot of frogs. Thank the Lord that was over twenty years ago. I know now that my actions were not pleasing and honoring to the Lord. Praise God, I am not the same person. "'Come now, and let us reason together,' says the Lord, 'though your sins are as scarlet, they will be as white as snow; though they are red like crimson, they will be like wool'" (Isaiah 1:18).

After I was saved, one of my greatest desires was to live a pure and holy life—the two always go together. I made up my mind and started a pursuit of studying God's Word. God said of the church, "He might sanctify her, having cleansed her by the washing of water with the word, that He might present to Himself the church in all her glory, having no spot or wrinkle or any such thing; but that she would be holy and blameless" (Ephesians 5:26–27).

I stopped kissing—I stopped it all. These are my convictions. My mother used to tell me, "Why light a fire if you have to put it out?" Not only is this true, but I believe I am to honor and glorify the Lord in every area of my life. If I date anyone, he must honor and agree with my decisions concerning a pure lifestyle prior to marriage. He must have the same convictions that I do. If he doesn't, I'm not interested! You may think that is too radical. But I know this is how the Lord wants me to live.

Seek the Lord. What do you think He is telling you to

do? Anything that goes against what He says in His Word is *not* from God. I have heard some pretty amazing stories from people who said, "God told me it was all right" . . . but their compromises are far from what God says. If you believe anything that is contrary to the Bible, God did not say it—you are rationalizing what you know is wrong. I realize this sounds simplistic, but I am amazed at people who say they are Christians but continue to sleep around, continue to live with their boyfriends, continue to be immoral in every way—and they expect God to bless their lives.

Maybe you have kept your virginity, but your mind is full of lust. You may push it to the limit in every other sexual way. Do believe God is honored with this? How do you dress? Often one's outward appearance can depict what's on the inside. When I go work out at the sports club, I am amazed at how little women are wearing. It appears they are there for more than just exercise; it looks as though they are trying to attract a man.

I would hate to think that the only way I could get a date was to come across to a man as sexy. Yes, men may ask a woman out for that reason, but is this why most women want men interested in them? I have seen many women hurt, because after dating someone for a while, they believe that the man they are dating is only interested in one thing. But sometimes the woman first attracted the man by the sexy way she dressed.

Purity is not just abstaining from sex. It's in our countenance, it's in our wardrobe, it's in how we walk, it's in how we talk, it's in what we read, it's in what we watch, it's in who we're with, it's who we are. Who do you want to be?

No matter your past, no matter your present situation, you can live a pure, holy, righteous life that is pleasing to God. Start today! Radical changes may need to take place in your life, but purity is completely possible with the Lord. Yes, there will be times when you must die to your flesh. Over and over you must die. We live in this body of flesh, we have sinful desires, but we must not give in to these desires.

Recently, I had my annual physical. As I sat and answered questions from the nurse, she asked, "Now what kind of birth control do you use?" For some strange reason, I was shocked at the question. I thought, *Don't you see on my paperwork that I am not married?* I said, "Abstinence. I don't have sex." She answered, "That's the best form of birth control." I could tell from her voice that she rarely hears that from women. Unfortunately, many Christian women today place their standard for living on what the world says is acceptable.

People often use the excuse, "But you don't know my past." Or, "I have been married before. I did too much when I was younger, and I can't seem to get past that." Yes, anything we have experienced in life, anything we've tasted, we remember. Satan tries to use it against us. But God is greater. "Greater is He who is in you than he who is in the world" (1 John 4:4).

The Battle You Can Win

Has the world come in and influenced your thinking? Do you see yourself as part of "the world"? How are you living? Maybe you should examine your heart to see if you have truly been born again. Am I saying a Christian will not struggle at times or be tempted? No! The key is not giving in to the temptation. In our own strength, it is impossible. Daily walking and abiding in Christ is a must. Earnestly desire a completely surrendered life to purity. It is a choice, my friend, a choice to please God or to please yourself. If you still cannot get past this, consider talking to a godly counselor, a counselor of your same sex. Get help! Don't continue to live in sin.

If you're constantly battling with immoral activity, first examine what has gotten you there. The road to immorality begins with a progression of small compromises. If you are in a relationship with someone who is not treating you with the utmost respect, why are you involved with him? If he does not honor you in every area of your life, examine this relationship closely. Where is it headed, what future does it have? Maybe you think what the Bible says about sex is not for today. But God's Word never changes.

It is extremely important to hold on to God's precepts when the Enemy bombards your mind with lies, telling you, *It's OK to give in to your temptations.* I love the Psalms. These are great verses to cling to when you're feeling weak.

How can a young man keep his way pure? By keeping it according to Your word. With all my heart I have sought You; do not let me wander from Your commandments. Your word I have treasured in my heart, that I may not sin against You. Blessed are You, O Lord; teach me Your statutes. With my lips I have told of all the ordinances of Your mouth. I have rejoiced in the way of Your testimonies, as much as in all riches. I will meditate on Your precepts and regard Your ways. (Psalm 119:9–15)

You may feel as though you just cannot control yourself. The apostle Paul deals with this. He says, "Yet I wish that all men were even as I myself am. However, each man has his own gift from God, one in this manner, and another in that. But I say to the unmarried and to widows that it is good for them if they remain even as I. But if they do not have self-control, let them marry; for it is better to marry than to burn with passion" (1 Corinthians 7:7–9).

It's not the Lord's desire for you to be miserable, to just burn with passion. You need to first be sure that you have done everything possible not to trigger your passions. Everything. Quit looking at the magazines. Quit watching the sex-oriented TV shows and movies. Replace them with something wholesome.

Give it time. There were times that I would pray these verses back to the Lord. He helped me deal with my passions, even though I have no husband. But He may bring you a mate. Continue to pray, and seek Him.

Let me warn you—if you are sleeping around or doing any kind of immoral activity, sooner or later you *will* suffer grave consequences. I encourage you to examine who and what is determining your lifestyle. Is there anything in your life that you know is not pleasing to the Lord? I beg you not to play with any kind of immorality. Don't think you can play with fire and not get burned! *Run* from it.

"Flee from youthful lusts and pursue righteousness" (2 Timothy 2:22). Simple words, but so very, very true. But don't only run *from* the lustful things in your life; run *to* God.

Constantly fill your mind with His words. "Finally, brethren, whatever is true, whatever is honorable, whatever is right, whatever is pure, whatever is lovely, whatever is of good repute, if there is any excellence and if anything worthy of praise, dwell on these things" (Philippians 4:8).

It is imperative that you live by this verse if you desire a life of purity. Do you want clean, pure thoughts flooding your mind, or do you want your mind to be like a sewer of ugly, dirty garbage? What good could possibly come from this?

No matter what your past has been, today is a brand-new day. Don't you love new beginnings, fresh new starts! I believe if you truly want to be obedient to God's Word, you don't have to stay frustrated over sexual decisions, because your standards will be formed by God's Word and decisions will be made ahead of time. It's certainly not a matter of how far you can push sexual activity and "get away with it"; it's a matter of holiness.

You have to make up your mind that this is what you want. You have to determine in your heart that you simply do not have a choice. A good example of this is seen in the book of Daniel. "But Daniel made up his mind that he would not defile himself with the king's choice food or with the wine which he drank; so he sought permission from the commander of the officials that he might not defile himself" (Daniel 1:8). Daniel made up his mind *ahead of time.* Have you?

Maybe you have never been tempted in the area of sex, or you think you have overcome sexual sins. I would encourage you to never, ever let your guard down. Do not put yourself in a position where you know you will be tempted. The Lord called David a man after His own heart. Yet David ended up being a man who committed adultery, got a woman pregnant, then murdered to cover up his sin. What happened to David?

We read in 2 Samuel 11:1–5:

> Then it happened in the spring, at the time when kings go out to battle, that David sent Joab and his servants with him and all Israel, and they destroyed the sons of Ammon and besieged Rabbah. But David stayed at Jerusalem. Now when evening came David arose from his bed and walked around on the roof of the king's house, and from the roof he saw a woman bathing; and the woman was very beautiful in appearance. So David sent and inquired about the woman. And one said, "Is this not Bathsheba, the daughter of Eliam, the wife of Uriah the Hittite?" David sent messengers and took her, and when she came to him, he lay with her; and when she had purified herself from her uncleanness, she returned to her house. The woman conceived; and she sent and told David, and said, "I am pregnant."

How could this be? How could David have done this? God's Word clearly shows us the mistakes David made.

Often we can miss the significance of well-known Bible stories. One very dangerous aspect that has come from the life of David is that some people use David's sin as an excuse for their own sin. People have said, "If a godly man like David cannot stay pure, how do you expect me to?" Satan would certainly have you twist this story to fit your reasons to choose to sin.

Consider how David could have avoided all that happened to him. Two major problems: David should have been at war (2 Samuel 11:1), and he looked upon Bathsheba.

These two things are extremely important: David wasn't where he should have been, and he was doing something he shouldn't have been doing. If you intend to live a pure, godly lifestyle, what can you learn from David's life? It is very important that you are living in the center of God's will. Often in life we get lazy, and maybe we don't want to go and be where God wants us. Remember David—he needed to be at war, but he chose to stay home.

We also read that David "saw a woman bathing, and she was very beautiful in appearance." David saw a woman bathing—this became his problem. What we let our eyes see is critical to walking and living a pure and holy life. Closely examine your temptations. What you let your eyes see makes an enormous difference.

The Necessity of Guarding Your Mind

I have made it a point not to read romance novels or look at dirty magazines. To my disappointment, immoral images came straight into my home without me asking for them. Through the years, I noticed a big change in what was being aired on basic cable TV. One evening I was flipping the channels, and unfortunately I stopped on the crudest X-rated program I have ever seen. After a couple of minutes I changed the channel. But a couple of minutes of that was more than enough to fill my mind with filthy thoughts for a lifetime. I was terribly upset.

The next day I called my local cable service and told them about this, but they had no idea what it was or where it came from. I let it pass and thought it was just a bad mistake. I later began flipping the channels again and came across more sensual perversion. I could not figure out how this could be allowed on the basic cable system. Unfortunately, I had seen enough that it became a stronghold in my mind, and the images that I let in hindered pure thoughts.

I can remember praying one day, and clearly the Lord gave me the verse, "If your eye causes you to stumble, pluck it out" (Matthew 18:9a). I knew then that I was to take out these cable channels. I once again called my cable service and asked if they could take out certain channels and let me keep the ones I enjoyed. They said they could not, so I told them to take them all. I now have a basic cable service with about sixteen channels. Yes, I gave up some of my favorite programming, but I have never been sorry. The Lord will always honor our obedience.

I also know that I can never open the door to anything on the Internet. I have determined to *never* go to an immoral Website. Have you made the same decision?

You must make strong decisions about what you will let your eyes see. At the end of a workweek, I enjoy going to see a good movie. As I pick up the newspaper and see what movies are playing, often I am disappointed. The movie reviews frequently say, "Sex, violence, language, nudity," and once again I have to choose another form of entertainment.

With all the bombardment from the world, we almost have to be like the mule that has blinders on because it is the best and safest way to walk. You're walking in the midst of the dark, but by looking straight ahead at Jesus and not at what is all around you, you're walking in the light!

I Just Want Somebody to Love Me

All too often for women it's not about sex, it's about love. We just want to be loved, and unfortunately somewhere in desiring this love, this attention, having some sort of romance, it goes past true love and becomes something we never wanted it to be. A woman can never bring back her virginity, but instead of stopping this lifestyle, Satan comes in and convinces her that she has already lost something very special, so why not continue? Has he ever told you this lie? Jesus has a better plan.

Jesus dealt beautifully with a woman who was desperately looking for love. She went from man to man, but was never fulfilled. My heart breaks as I see women today doing the same thing. A woman convinces herself that if she goes to bed with the man who is giving her attention that maybe, just maybe, he will love her. Maybe then they will get married. But, the pain in her heart grows strong, the quest continues . . . and her life remains empty. And then Jesus enters.

The woman said to him, "Sir, give me this water so that I won't get thirsty and have to keep coming here to draw water." He told her, "Go, call your husband and come back." "I have no husband," she replied. Jesus said to her, "You are right when you say you have no husband. The fact is, you have had five husbands, and the man you now have is not your husband." (John 4:15–18 NIV)

This same story has been told concerning countless women who just want to be loved. They cannot find a husband, so why not settle for what they can have? Is this really love?

Remember, we can all fall, anytime, anywhere—never think any differently! Healing of sexual sin is very important. Godly counsel and support are a must. Pray and seek whom the Lord would have you talk with. Jesus says to "confess your sins to one another" (James 5:16). Be discreet, pray, and talk privately with mature, godly counsel. Run! Get help—do whatever it takes, but start today!

Sex outside of marriage will never satisfy. The desire may be great, but God's plan is for sex only to be in marriage. God says, "Marriage is to be held in honor among all, and the marriage bed is to be undefiled; for fornicators and adulterers God will judge" (Hebrews 13:4).

God's way is always best.

Today, unfortunately, many have chosen to live in sexual immorality. The devastation of this sin continues to rip the very fabric of our great nation. But many are choosing to live a pure and holy life. What about you?

Whatever you have been through, always remember

that God forgives. No matter your past, He has a wonderful future for you as you give it all up for Him. Let Him be
the lover of your soul, and you will never be sorry.

NOTE

1. Henry J. Rogers, *The Silent War: Ministering to Those Trapped in the Deception of Pornography* (Green Forest, Alaska: New Leaf, 2000), 138.

▨ ▨ ▨ ▨ ▨ ▨ ▨ ▨ ▨ ▨ ▨ ▨ ▨ ▨ ▨ ▨

Passion That
Makes a Difference

▨ ▨ ▨ ▨ ▨ ▨ ▨ ▨ ▨ ▨ ▨ ▨ ▨ ▨ ▨ ▨

Have you ever heard anyone say, "If I just had more passion in my life, then maybe I could be happy"?

Can you imagine Hollywood ever producing a film with a love story that didn't have passion? Take Clark Gable and Vivien Leigh in *Gone with the Wind*—now, there was passion! It seems that every Academy Award winner has passion. With today's movies flooding the screens, often wives are unhappy because of their husbands' lack of romance, lack of passion. Singles, too, become very unhappy because they don't have passion in their lives.

When you hear the word *passion*, is your first thought romance or sex? Our culture has inundated our minds with images of beautiful women and handsome men. Many Americans put every ounce of effort into beautifying their bodies in order to emulate the images they have seen on the big screen. Their aim is to have a gorgeous, tanned body. Their deeper desire . . . passion!

As singles, we may feel that if our bodies were just in better physical shape, then surely someone would love us and we could have this kind of passion. It is amazing to see the continual increase in book sales on diets and exercise. I often wonder how many we can have, but every year there seems to be some kind of new diet. Surely there will be one that will beat all the others, we think. Yes, it gets my attention, and I usually purchase the latest book out.

Everywhere we look there are health and fitness clubs, beauty spas, and tanning salons. This obsession with the human body certainly is nothing new. The Greek and Roman empires loved the body. Some of the most recognized Greek sculptures are statues of the human body.

Many people today are also obsessed with their bodies, but what is their motive? Could they believe the perfect body will give them the perfect passion and romance, and life will be everything they hoped it would be? Certainly we need to be concerned how we treat our bodies. Unfortunately, some Christians don't see the importance of a healthy diet and exercise.

Our bodies are the temples of God, and we are a testimony in everything we do and in how we look. In the book of 1 Corinthians we read, "Do you not know that you are a temple of God and that the Spirit of God dwells in you? If any man destroys the temple of God, God will destroy him, for the temple of God is holy, and that is what you are" (3:16–17). We also see in 1 Corinthians 10:31, "Whether, then, you eat or drink or whatever you do, do all to the glory of God."

How we treat our bodies is important to God. But even if I could obtain the perfect body and the Lord brought me a wonderful, godly husband, and even if we were extremely passionate and madly in love with each other, would my life be perfect?

How many couples do you know who hadn't been married long before you could tell that something was wrong? Your friends, who were newlyweds, came back to the office, and the once elated smile had become a solemn look. You think, *The honeymoon is over.* We have all seen it. What happens? Where is the passion?

I am in no way demeaning or putting down marriage. Nor am I trying to suggest that wonderful passion and sex cannot continue throughout a marriage—this is God's plan.

What I want you to consider is that you can have all the romantic passion in the world, but sexual passion by itself doesn't keep a married couple content and happy—and sex outside of marriage never brings lasting happiness. Many eventually continue their pursuit for more passion, better sex, and often they leave their mates to find it. What happens? We read about the Hollywood stars who can't seem to stay together, yet it appears that they would have all the elements for having the perfect passion. But, even with all the glitz and glamour, the perfect bodies, beauty in their lives, it's still never enough.

Passion—Who Has It?

Why do we so often think of the word *passion* in the context of romance and sex? Webster defines passion as "suffering, as of a martyr; the suffering of Jesus during the Crucifixion or after the Last Supper; any emotion, as hate, grief, love, etc.; all of these emotions; extreme emotion; specif., a) rage, fury, b) enthusiasm [a passion for music], c) strong love or affection, d) sexual desire, lust; the object of strong desire or fondness."[1]

What are you passionate about? Does it make a difference in your life? Passion that is targeted and focused has been used to build empires, win wars, fight segregation, put a man on the moon, and journey across an unknown sea to discover a land now called America.

Have you ever watched anyone in leadership try to lead a country, a company, or a church without passion? Without passion, how does one lead? Not very well! Passion is vital!

Imagine a man with little formal education. While growing up, his major chores were to become efficient at using an ax and to make fence rails by splitting poles. And wonder of wonders, a rail-splitter became the sixteenth president of the United States—Abraham Lincoln, a true man of *passion*.

Maybe you are one God has chosen to go and do what no one has done before. But your continual search for this physical, intimate, sexual passion in wrong relationships, or even your preoccupation with getting married, has kept you from being and doing all that God has designed for you. Turn away from any sin in your life that has held you captive! Run to the living and true God, who can change your life for His purposes. Let God give you the passion you need to make a difference in our world.

Redirect your lack of a physical passion in relationships by "lov[ing] the Lord your God with all your heart, and with all your soul, and with all your mind, and with all your strength" (Mark 12:30)—this is passion. Give every bit of yourself to God. There is no better passion on earth. No greater blessing, no better love.

Where is your heart? Your heart is what motivates and influences the decisions in your life. I believe an important verse for everyone, especially singles, is Proverbs 4:23, "Watch over your heart with all diligence, for from it flow the springs of life." Guard your heart; it is critical to all your decisions. Why? An unguarded heart has ofen resulted in wrong marriages, unwanted pregnancies, and lost purity.

A Passion for God

Often we get on this treadmill called life, and we don't slow down long enough to think about what is driving us. Where is your focus? What do you think about? What do you dream about? These thoughts, these dreams, often may be what is shaping and forming your life. Where are they taking you? What are you doing for the kingdom of God? Is your life making an eternal difference?

Every minute of every day is being spent on yourself or on others. Are you influencing lives for good or evil? It is very easy, if we are not careful, to become self-absorbed.

Unfortunately, we are living in an incredibly selfish society. Does it look good, feel good, and taste good? For many there are no standards. I am amazed at how spoiled our affluent society has made us. Cash is available to us almost anywhere, at any time. We have so many choices . . . I want my latté decaffeinated, with skim milk, vanilla flavoring, and a touch of cinnamon.

We don't want much, do we? We want our clothes dry-cleaned in twenty-four hours. The average restaurant must be able to serve a full-course meal in less than ten minutes. It must look good, certainly must taste good, and cannot cost too much.

Our culture must compete in the world of excellence. Many of our shopping malls have become quite beautiful, with the finest stores to meet our every desire. The highly glossed wooden floors, the perfectly designed store windows, and wonderful coffee and cookies are offered as we shop. Who can resist? With all the extravagance and wealth that many Americans experience, how has our world been affected?

Who wants to be a millionaire? This obsession to become rich has inundated our culture. The casinos and gambling clubs are ever increasing, and it still doesn't seem to be enough. Reality TV programs are the rage, and again focus on the common theme for many of "get rich quick." Those who appear on these programs often lose all self-respect . . . many not seeming to care that the world is watching their every move. Some are even involved in sexual activity, knowing every TV viewer in America can watch. This should frighten us to the very core of our being.

Our world has left the standards God set for us. The true pulse of our nation appears to be a passion for pleasure, outside every guideline God ordained. It has become an obsession. Far too many people believe that money and sex are the way to real happiness. What has happened to the heart of a nation that was founded on God's principles, God's precepts?

Several years ago something very strange seemed to be happening with my heart. For no apparent reason it would start racing, even if I were only sitting or lying on the sofa. I decided to see a doctor about this, and I was given an echocardiogram. The nurse who gave me the test said, "This is great; I have a very good picture of your heart." I thought, *But how is my heart?* It was fine. The occasional change in heart rhythm went away in time.

Today I would love to be able to take a picture of your heart. What would the picture show? You may be in a very difficult season in your life. You are hurting, your heart is breaking. Since your heart drives your emotions, your thinking, your decisions, it is very important to know the condition of your heart. Despite the circumstances that have hurt you, do you still trust God? Do you want to make a difference in our world? Is your number-one priority in life to love, honor, and obey God? God says, "For the eyes of the Lord move to and fro throughout the earth that He may strongly support those whose heart is completely His" (2 Chronicles 16:9). A heart that is completely His. . . . Is it your passion in life to have this kind of heart?

God says, "If you love Me, you will keep My commandments" (John 14:15). The immoral deeds of the flesh are obvious (Galatians 5:19). A person who is listening, obeying, and walking with God is one who is in step with God's purpose and plan for his or her life.

Is your passion for God growing greater? A passion for God will create in you other strong passions.

Passion for People

Have you met Christians who act hateful? I have. They can do so much harm to the church of God. As Christians we are to walk and live by the Spirit. "The fruit of the Spirit is love, joy, peace, patience, kindness, goodness, faithfulness, gentleness, self-control" (Galatians 5:22).

If you live this kind of life, people are drawn to you. But if you live in a state of continual self-pity because you have never been married, or you are divorced, or you are a single mom, continue to seek God. Often when we get our minds off ourselves and onto others, it can make a tremendous difference. Whatever your situation may be, whatever your pain, God can use you for His glory.

Be very careful not to compare your hurt or your heartbreak to that of other people. It may appear that the pain you have experienced is a lot more agonizing than the hurts you see in others, but we can never truly know the pain and heartache someone else has experienced or is feeling. Ask God to use your pain. You have a greater understanding of how others may feel because of it. You can sympathize with their hurts, their suffering. What is the Christian life if it is not to live for others?

I have a friend who never dreamed she would not be

married and have children. All of her siblings are married with children. She could choose to let this defeat her and question God, wondering why He didn't do the same for her. But she chooses to spend quality time with her nieces and nephews. She also is a gifted teacher, and she pours much of her life into teaching preschoolers at her church. Children love her. She has not only filled a void in her life, but she also is making a difference in the lives of many children.

"If I speak with the tongues of men and of angels, but do not have love, I have become a noisy gong or a clanging cymbal" (1 Corinthians 13:1). I will never forget when I heard a pastor speak on this verse. He walked up to the podium with a bunch of tin cans tied together on a string. He started banging all the cans together. It was loud, and he kept making it louder and louder. He finally stopped. This was a great illustration of our lives without love. Without love, we turn people off. They want us to be quiet . . . and they certainly don't want to be around us.

The apostle Paul had an enormous amount of love for people. He said, "I thank God, whom I serve with a clear conscience the way my forefathers did, as I constantly remember you in my prayers night and day, longing to see you, even as I recall your tears, so that I may be filled with joy" (2 Timothy 1:3–4).

Paul was a man of passion, a man of love for people. He wrote these words as he sat in a prison cell. His mind was not on his circumstances, but on others. He was a man with great concern for people. Paul went on to say to Timothy:

For I am mindful of the sincere faith within you, which first dwelt in your grandmother Lois and your mother Eunice, and I am sure that it is in you as well. For this reason I remind you to kindle afresh the gift of God which is in you through the laying on of my hands. For God has not given us a spirit of timidity, but of power and love and discipline. Therefore do not be ashamed of the testimony of our Lord or of me His prisoner, but join with me in suffering for the gospel according to the power of God, who has saved us. (2 Timothy 1:5–9)

In these few short verses Paul was reminding Timothy to "kindle afresh the gift of God which is in [him]." Every believer, every child of God, has been given spiritual gifts. The gifts God has given you will become your passion in life, and through these gifts you should have another new passion.

Passion for Service

One of the greatest studies you can ever do will be on spiritual gifts. Paul tells us that we are to know and understand the gifts. First Corinthians 12:1 says, "Now concerning spiritual gifts, brethren, I do not want you to be unaware." Knowing and understanding your gifts not only will help give you great direction for your life, but also will free you to do what God has called you to do.

"Now there are varieties of gifts, but the same Spirit. And there are varieties of ministries, and the same Lord. There are varieties of effects, but the same God who works all things in all persons. But to each one is given the manifestation of the Spirit for the common good" (1 Corinthians 12:4–7).

As you study the gifts of the Spirit, you will see that not everyone needs to teach, or preach, or be a deacon. If the church is working together as God has designed and planned, it is a perfect picture of the body. Not everyone is a hand, an eye, or a foot. But the body needs every part. You are needed greatly in the body of Christ. Are you using your gifts? Are you serving in your church?

One of my greatest passions in life is to share the Gospel with unbelievers. I also love to teach and encourage others. Through the years it has become obvious that two of my gifts are exhortation and evangelism. As the Scripture mentions, many of us will have the same gifts, but different ministries. I have a passion to teach women, not children. Many at my church laugh if they see me helping with the preschoolers (which is rare), because they know that on that day there was no other choice than to grab me and use me to fill in.

There will be times that you will need to get out of your comfort zone. You may need to help clean the church, work with children, or cook a meal. Don't use the excuse, "It's not my gift." Beyond giving us specific gifts, God also calls us to be servants. Simply do what He tells you to do.

What do you desire to do? What are you passionate about? If you could do anything, what would it be? Ask God to show you. He has gifted you like no one else. He wants to use all your past, all your life experiences, everything, for His glory. He has molded, shaped, created you for a purpose—His purpose.

One of my favorite movies is *Chariots of Fire*. In 1981, this low-budget British film surprised everyone by winning four Academy Awards, including "Best Picture." *Chariots of Fire* was a captivating movie about the lives of men who ran in the 1924 Olympics. As I watched this movie, one man stood out among them all, Eric Liddell.

Eric was a man with true convictions. After all the dogged determination to do his very best, the ruthless workouts and training to make it to the Olympics, he received the news that the 100-meter heats would be run on Sunday. "Eric believed the Christian Sabbath belonged to God and was to be kept as a day of worship and rest. Many devout Scots of the day held the same non-negotiable conviction about Sunday, but none of them was favored to win the 100 meters in the coming Olympics."[2]

Yes, much of the world knew about Eric because he was a gold medallist. But I believe we're still talking about him today not for his medal, but because of his relentless desire to please the Lord with every ounce of his being. Instead of resting on his athletic fame, he ended his days as a missionary in China, out of obedience to God's call on His life. Eric Liddell was a true man of passion!

God made Eric fast, and Eric "felt His pleasure" as he ran because he was doing exactly what God had called him to do at that time in his life. Is God's call on your life? Do you feel His pleasure?

Do you have a passion for God, for people, and for His service? If you are living the Christian life as He intends you to do, you will feel His pleasure. Do you sense God's power, His supernatural touch on your life? There is absolutely nothing better in all the world than knowing you are in right standing with God and doing what He has created you to do.

NOTES

1. *Webster's New World Dictionary* (Nashville: The South Western Company, 1974), 546.
2. David McCasland, *Eric Liddell: Pure Gold* (Grand Rapids: Discovery House, 2001), 77.

The Surprise Gift

Don't you love gifts? Some of the best gifts I have ever received were complete surprises. Gifts come in all shapes and sizes, but often it can be the surprise gifts we like the best. No one is more surprised than I am that I believe my singleness is a gift from the Lord.

Before you shut the book or decide to skip this chapter, please consider that this could be true. I certainly understand what you may be feeling. I can remember when it would almost make me angry if I heard a teacher or pastor talk about singleness as being a gift. The last thing I wanted to hear from anyone was that any part of singleness could be a gift. After hearing that, it was difficult to listen to anything else the person had to say. I would start my list of all the reasons I thought it was not only good to be married, but *better*.

Therefore, before I lose you completely, read on and see if you can understand why I think the way I do.

First, the Bible does not contain a formal definition of a "gift of singleness." Nowhere does any biblical writer clearly say anything like "The gift of singleness means that God makes you happy without marriage." The only reference to such a gift is found in Paul's words in 1 Corinthians 7:7: "I wish that all were as I myself am. But each has a particular gift from God, one having one kind and another a different kind" (NRSV).[1]

For years I thought I would be married; therefore, I believed I did not have the "gift of singleness." I never *felt* like I had this gift. But is this verse talking about how I *feel?* What images or thoughts come to mind when you think of a person having this gift? I can easily picture an old movie where the priest is dressed in his long robe, briskly walking through dark hallways, carrying his dimly lit candle as he heads toward the chapel to pray his 4:00 A.M. prayers. Now, if this is someone with the gift of singleness, it certainly could not be me! But could I have this gift and not *feel* like it?

Could it be that being single is not the life you feel like having? Is it possible to move past this? I never thought I could relate to Paul when he says, "I wish that all were as I myself am." Paul was a man who had such a passion to reach others for the Gospel of Jesus Christ that he was very content in his singleness.

Often it can feel strange to be single in what appears to be a couples world, but remember you must walk in the truths of what you know, not in how you feel. Understanding the Scriptures should liberate you to choose to be content if you are single—the Lord has given you enough grace to be single. Can you accept for today your singleness as a gift from the Lord? Or does it continue to make you angry? Do you keep saying, "But I don't want that gift"?

I will never forget when someone said those words to me. A dear friend of mine had just given birth to her third baby, and I thought it might be nice to take her baby a gift. As I was shopping for just the right outfit, it came to mind that I should pick up something for her other two children. Now, I am not a mother, but I have seen kids get pretty jealous of the new baby who has just arrived and changed their whole world.

I went to several stores trying to find some kind of small, cute little toy for my friend's four-year-old daughter and three-year-old son. I was proud of myself as I selected my gifts for her children. I couldn't wait to see their expressions as I gave them their gifts.

Unfortunately, I was not quite prepared for the response I got. The baby's gift was greatly appreciated. But my friend's son was playing and was not really interested in receiving his gift at the time. I thought her daughter would be surprised and thrilled that I had brought her something. She came running into the living room, intently looking up at me, smiling from ear to ear, holding out her hands in great anticipation for what I had brought her.

I was hiding the gifts (two adorable little stuffed animals, a cow and a horse) behind my back. When I showed them to her with great joy and expectation, her mouth dropped to a frown, and she said, "I don't like Beanie Babies, but I will take them." She was very unhappy with her gift.

Do you feel that way about your singleness? Have you been wearing a frown for a very long time? Do you think your heavenly Father has not given you the very best gift? Oh, my friend, how I understand. There have been periods in my life when I didn't like being single. I wasted precious time waiting for something different, hoping for something different from the life the Lord had given me.

Paul's life was so focused that he didn't have time to sit around thinking about his singleness. He was truly content. Don't you picture a person who loves life, loves God, and loves his singleness? Not only does Paul say, "I wish that all were as I myself am," but he goes on to say:

> But I want you to be free from concern. One who is unmarried is concerned about the things of the Lord, how he may please the Lord; but one who is married is concerned about the things of the world, how he may please his wife, and his interests are divided. (1 Corinthians 7:32–34a)

You may be thinking, "That's Paul, and I will surely never think like that." Keep in mind that there is nothing wrong with you if you desire to be married. Certainly for most this is the norm. But if you are single today, how are you living? Can you accept the place where God has you at this time?

> There is an appointed time for everything. And there is a time for every event under heaven—a time to give birth and a time to die; a time to plant and a time to uproot what is planted. A time to kill and a time to heal; a time to tear

down and a time to build up. A time to weep and a time to laugh; a time to mourn and a time to dance. (Ecclesiastes 3:1–4)

How I wish I could tell you that you can wake up tomorrow and your strong desire to be married or have children will have gone away. I can't. But I can tell you it will get better if you truly surrender to the Lord. If everything in you wants to live a life that glorifies Him, you will find joy.

Just as the Father has loved Me, I have also loved you; abide in My love. If you keep My commandments, you will abide in My love; just as I have kept My Father's commandments and abide in His love. These things I have spoken to you so that My joy may be in you, and that your joy may be made full. (John 15:9–11)

Trying to live this life of singleness—or any other kind of life—other than in God's power, and by His love and grace, will make you empty and dissatisfied. The void will always be there.

I can honestly say that I am happier today than I have ever been in my life—though I still have no husband or children, both of which I had thought would bring me the greatest joy. How did I get past this? It may appear too hard, but honestly it is simply daily walking, daily abiding, daily dying to self—and daily growing in Him. Give it time.

Don't lose heart—it will get better. Hang on . . . hang on to Him. Pour out your heart to Him. Tell Him your

I Kissed a Lot of Frogs

frustrations, tell Him your longings, ask Him to change your heart. That's what I did—as I continued to struggle with the fact that I didn't have a husband, I began crying out to the Lord to change my heart . . . for His plans for my life to become my desires . . . and it happened.

The Advantage of Freedom

Today, not only do I feel truly complete in Him, I feel very, very *free*. Begin to change your paradigm, how you look at your singleness. Do you continually dwell on the fact that you are single? Do you read romance novels, go to movies with love stories, hang out with couples who can't seem to keep their hands off each other? Now, if I have heavy doses of these things, yes, I can quickly get very depressed. Refocus—refocus—refocus! Focus on what you *do* have!

Start counting your blessings. Sometimes when I start to have a little pity party, I have to remind myself to count my blessings. I make myself say ten things out loud for which I am grateful. Try it! It works!

You might still be saying, "I cannot think of one good thing about being single." Let's look again at what Paul said to the Corinthians concerning marriage and singleness.

But I want you to be free from concern. One who is unmarried is concerned about the things of the Lord, how he may please the Lord; but one who is married is concerned about the things of the world, how he may please his wife, and his interests are divided. (1 Corinthians 7:32–34a)

104

As I read these verses, there are three very important words that leap off the page: *"free from concern."* You are *free!* If you cannot think of anything good about being single, dwell on your freedom for just a little while. It's as though I see Paul saying, "Can you hear me? Think about what you're getting into here by getting married! Think . . . You're losing your freedom! You will soon become concerned about many things . . . your husband, your children. Your freedom has now turned into *great* concern."

Those of you who are single moms have the added responsibility of raising children. Do all that you can to lay your burdens, your cares, at God's feet. Many of you may feel overwhelmed with the tremendous weight of raising children alone. It helps to "[cast] all your anxiety on Him, because He cares for you" (1 Peter 5:7). Let God help you carry the load.

For a period in my life, I attended a small prayer group on Monday nights. During this time I had gone through a number of very disappointing relationships. We all talked about the difficulties we were going through. Quite often I heard about extremely difficult situations going on in marriages. It seemed to happen week after week. I would leave thinking that my singleness problems paled to those in these marriages.

We often seem to think that life will be better after marriage. I have thought that tomorrow would be better than today, especially if I had a husband. I used to think I would wait to do certain things until after I had a husband. I waited a number of years before ever buying a nice big bed. I thought this is what you did when you got engaged—

you and the one you loved picked out the bed you would sleep in together for the rest of your life. I finally realized how silly that was.

I also used to think it was best to be married to take certain vacations. That was ridiculous thinking! I have been to a number of countries all over the world, and I didn't need a husband to go with me. I had a wonderful time!

Maybe you're waiting to purchase a home because you feel that this is admitting that you will stay single. This is not true. I have a friend who decided to purchase a house, and just a few months after buying it, she got engaged and is now married. You should at least consider saving for a home, even if now is not the time to purchase one. Seek the Lord about what He would have you do in this area; He's the only one who knows your future.

Maybe there are other things in your life that you have on hold, and you're waiting for a mate to come in order to do them. Obviously sex must be put on hold, but consider all the other things that you can do because you are single!

Our Numbered Days

The older I am, the more precious life is to me. Life consists of years, months, days, hours that I am alive. As long as I have breath, I have life on this earth. Each passing hour, minute, second equals *time.*

How are you spending your time? Don't waste it waiting, wondering, for the moment you will be married. Use the freedom God has given you for Him. Make the most of the time while you are single.

Some live in the past, some live in the future, and some live for today. Don't miss life; don't let it pass you by. I love this quote by Jim Elliott: "Wherever you are, be all there."

Live! You may not have tomorrow. Don't miss "the gift"; don't hope for something else. Cherish it, be grateful for it. The Giver knows exactly the kind of gift you need for today. Paul eloquently described contentment in the book of Philippians. He wrote:

> The things you have learned and received and heard and seen in me, practice these things, and the God of peace will be with you. But I rejoiced in the Lord greatly, that now at last you have revived your concern for me; indeed, you were concerned before, but you lacked opportunity. Not that I speak from want, for I have learned to be content in whatever circumstances I am. I know how to get along with humble means, and I also know how to live in prosperity; in any and every circumstance I have learned the secret of being filled and going hungry, both of having abundance and suffering need. I can do all things through Him who strengthens me (Philippians 4:9–13)

It's only in God's strength that we walk this single life. So often we want simple answers for our singleness. Numerous people have said to me, "Don't lose faith, God can still bring you a mate." Yes, God can bring me a mate. The God of the universe who created the heavens and the earth can certainly bring me a husband if He so chooses. I am absolutely sure of that. If you are single, no matter your age, your background, your situation—if God wants you to be married, you will be. Give it time. But don't wait until marriage to start life.

Is your life on hold? Don't miss the *freedom* God has given you for today. No, God has not given you this freedom to waste. I have married friends who tell me they wish they had spent their time during their singleness serving the Lord instead of simply waiting for a husband. Is your life making a difference? Are you living purposefully for Him? Does your life bring honor to Him? Are you excited knowing that you can make a difference? Have you touched someone's life today?

There are countless ways in which the Lord may choose to use you. We are not all called to be missionaries in Africa, but right where you live could be the very place God has chosen for you to serve. A changed life for the kingdom of God is one of the greatest things that can happen to a person. Do you truly want to make a difference in other people's lives? I can think of no higher calling.

I enjoy every ounce of my freedom. It truly is a gift! As I sit and write this, I am sitting in a chalet, looking out at the great mountains of east Tennessee, listening to the rushing water of a creek outside my window. It is spectacular, it is perfect, and it's peaceful. Today I am free, and I love it!

NOTE

1. Albert Y. Hsu, *Singles at the Crossroads: A Fresh Perspective on Christian Singleness* (Downers Grove, Ill.: InterVarsity, 1997), 49.

Why Are Singles Misunderstood?

Has anyone ever said to you, "I cannot believe you are not married!" If you've been single for very long, you may have heard this and many other comments like it. Have you heard, "I guess there is no one good enough for you. Now, you can't be so picky; no one is perfect. You need to realize that everyone has flaws. Marriage is not always a honeymoon, but you had better not wait too long. You just have to jump in. You know, marriage is God's design."

Why are singles so misunderstood?

Why would anyone think that just because you are single you do not know that God instituted marriage? The Bible is clear concerning God's design for marriage. From the very beginning . . .

God created man in His own image, in the image of God He created him; male and female He created them. God blessed them; and God said to them, "Be fruitful and multiply, and fill the earth, and subdue it; and rule over the fish of the sea and over the birds of the sky and over every living thing that moves on the earth." (Genesis 1:27–28)

Later, in Genesis 2, we read:

The Lord God said, "It is not good for the man to be alone; I will make him a helper suitable for him." . . . So the Lord God caused a deep sleep to fall upon the man, and he slept; then He took one of his ribs and closed up the flesh at that place. The Lord God fashioned into a woman the rib which He had taken from the man, and brought her to the man. The man said, "This is now bone of my bones, and flesh of my flesh; she shall be called Woman, because she was taken out of Man." For this reason a man shall leave his father and his mother, and be joined to his wife; and they shall become one flesh. (Genesis 2:18, 21–24)

Yes, marriage is God's design. But with all the verses in the Bible concerning marriage, does this mean His will is for every adult to be married? Obviously everyone is single at some point in his life. The Scriptures tell about some who were widowed and some who never married. Just to name a few, Naomi, Ruth, Jeremiah, Daniel, Paul, and Jesus were all single. Naomi and Ruth were widowed, and Ruth later remarried.

It should be comforting to see that being married has no bearing on spiritual maturity. It is obvious after looking at the Scriptures that God is not trying to punish those who are single. We can place much guilt on ourselves, questioning God concerning our singleness. But often it is what others think about us that can be so frustrating, so difficult, so hurtful.

You may be single and perfectly contented, so why can't others accept you that way? In order to obtain a better understanding of what singles feel, I talked with single women and asked a number of different women all across the country their thoughts about being single. Many of the same responses came my way concerning how they have been misunderstood.

Some Married Couples Don't Seem to Understand

Here are a few of the comments from singles about how they have been misunderstood by those who are married:

- *They cannot believe I can truly have a full, contented life without a husband.*

- *Until I get married I must be wild and carefree and could not possibly have any real responsibilities.*

- *People really have asked, "What do you do with all your spare time? What do you do on the weekends?"*

- *Many couples don't typically socialize with singles because they think they don't have anything in common, or they are afraid the single person will go after their mate.*

- *All singles are looking (just waiting) for the right mate to come along in order to finally start living life to the fullest.*

- *People assume that I am not domestic, that I cannot cook, that I eat out all the time.*

- *In most people's minds, it goes against the norm not to be married. They think at least a single person needs to be dating and on the verge of marriage. (Now that is normal.)*

- *Something must be wrong with me. How can I live without having sex? I must secretly be gay.*

- *I must have chosen not to be married and I discourage men from being interested in me.*

Why the misconceptions, why the misunderstandings, why the wedge we so often have between the married world and singles?

Some of my best friends are married. As close as I am with my married friends, some have had some of these same misconceptions. Why? How we view others can often be based solely on our own experiences. Most who are married do not intend to hurt, harm, or discourage someone who is single—they simply cannot relate.

Couples that married young may have wondered why you aren't married. When they were young and single, they pursued getting married, found a husband or wife, and had children. Now they cannot figure out why you don't do the same thing. It worked for them; now just follow and do what they did. They don't seem to realize that most singles have tried, and many still hope to get married. Some who are married might not understand that you also may have a strong desire to be married and have children.

When I have expressed my challenges of being single to my married friends, they have developed a better understanding about my singleness. Communication between those who are single and those who are married helps bring a better awareness of the struggles singles face. You may want to give a copy of this book to some of your married friends who simply don't understand singles. But just as those who are married may have misconceptions concerning singles, singles also have incorrect thoughts about those who are married.

I cannot imagine my life without some of my married friends. They have told me that they don't want to spend all their time only with other couples. It's good to spend time with both married and single friends and family members.

Our world is rapidly changing. Often, being single, we feel alone in what appears to be a couples-dominated world, but the adult single population is ever increasing. Please know you're not alone.

I was shocked as I researched and saw what was happening in our country concerning marriage. According to the Rutgers University National Marriage Project Report, "Marriage as the basis of family life continues to decline in America. Since 1970 the rate of marriage has dropped by about one third, the out-of-wedlock birth ratio has climbed from 11% to 33% of all births, the divorce rate has doubled, and the number of people living together outside of marriage has grown by over 1000%."[1] And, as mentioned in the first chapter, 44 percent of American women are single.

In some ways this may be a comfort to know you are

not alone. At times you may feel isolated and different; but according to these statistics you are certainly not alone in your singleness. Still, it saddens me to see these numbers, and I know it grieves God's heart, because marriage has been God's plan from the very beginning.

Singles and the Church Can Be an Odd Couple

Some of the hardest times I have ever had were, yes, in the church. Hearing sermons, over and over, on marriage and the family at times has been painful. Certainly these messages are important, but in some ways I felt like I didn't exist.

You too may have had some of these same feelings, but once again we have to come back to what we know and not how we feel. I have received e-mails from single women who told me about their feelings and comments they have heard from those in the church.

- *She seems like such a sweet girl, but she must have some real problems I'm not aware of—something that makes her unbearable. Maybe that is why she is not married.*

- *If you're trying to find a husband, there are no singles here.*

- *I know God has a mate for you; you need to have more faith.*

- *God gives you the desires of your heart. Just be patient and He will give you a husband.*

- *The church today is made up of families and married people who have formed a "club," so to speak. Anyone who is single surely is an incomplete person until becoming normal, like they are, with a spouse and children. It's turned into a social gathering place rather than a house of worship for a living God.*

• *Being single should be one of the best times of our Christian faith, but the church acts as though we're the leftovers, just waiting around until God gives us someone to keep us company—then our lives will be complete.*

• *I meet so many insecure, unmarried Christian women these days. They've been battered by the world, shunned and abandoned because of the "social-ness" of the church. But even sadder is the fact that they associate the love of Jesus with the love of the church (or its lack).*

The church today needs to be a hospital for the hurting, a place of love and acceptance for everyone who enters. No matter their race, age, background, or marital status, people want to be a part of a loving, caring, sincere group of people.

Where you attend church is extremely important. No two churches are exactly alike; therefore, we must never judge the church simply on a few bad experiences. Just as every church is different, singles are all different. Certainly there is no question that we are to be involved in a church, as this is what God tells us to do. His Word says:

Let us hold fast the confession of our hope without wavering, for He who promised is faithful; and let us consider how to stimulate one another to love and good deeds, not forsaking our own assembling together, as is the habit of some, but encouraging one another; and all the more as you see the day drawing near. (Hebrews 10:23–24)

Maybe you're not in church because you can't find a church with which you're happy. Certainly, if you live in a small city, your choices may be slim. Could it be that God is calling you to make a difference in a church located in your community?

Satan has truly won if he keeps you away from church. Don't let him win! Yes, the church consists of people who are not perfect, and you may have been hurt. Your feelings are real, but it's vital to move on and get past your hurt. Don't use it as an excuse not to be in church.

If you are not a member of a local body of believers, I suggest that you pray that God will show you where He wants you to be. We are drawn to join different churches for various reasons. When I was in my early twenties, it was extremely important for me to go to a church that had a large young-adult singles ministry. I desperately needed to be around Christian singles. I now attend a different church that currently does not have a singles ministry. But it does have a wonderful, gifted, godly pastor; a fantastic worship leader and music program; solid Bible studies; and a place where I can serve. The staff has selected me for various leadership positions and encouraged me to use my spiritual gifts. Everyone is encouraged to get involved—young, old, single, and married.

The majority of our members are young married couples with children, and occasionally this can be awkward and difficult. The young mothers talk about their children and husbands, preschool, VBS, AWANA, and youth camps. Then there's the young-married Sunday school classes . . . much to hear about, and much to get used to being around when attending church. My church has a number of single women, which helps—but notice I said "women," not many single men!

Despite being uncomfortable at times, I love my church, and for today this is where God has me. I cannot imagine not being extremely involved in church. What about you? Maybe the Lord is nudging you to get involved with a singles group at a church. This could be a good way to meet a mate, but not necessarily. You may not like "singles groups." I understand. But don't sit at home alone unless you're happy doing so. If you have a need for Christian friends, this is another good reason for being in church. Get out and do things with couples, singles, others who may not be exactly like you. Expand your area of comfort. It may not feel good at first, but you may meet a potential husband, or you may find some friends for life.

Family Can Inflict Wounds as Well

I've been truly blessed with a family that does not pressure me to be married. My mother has encouraged, hoped, and dreamed that I would be, because she knew that was my desire; therefore, my wishes are her wishes. As I have changed, she has changed, and for that I am grateful.

I don't know what kind of upbringing you have had, what kind of parents you have, but regardless of your family, obviously you have to be the one making your own choices, your own decisions in life. Possibly some in your family put pressure on you to be married. Maybe your parents want grandchildren, and if you don't have children, they won't have grandkids. Ask yourself, "Whose life am I living?" Will you make the wrong choice to marry just to please your parents? Or will you wait and see what God wants you to do? Always remember, you will never, ever be sorry for obeying the Lord and waiting on Him.

Misconceptions brought by the family include . . .

- *My grandfather told me, "You are not fulfilling your life as a woman if you do not marry and bear children. . . . Why do you think God put you here?"*

- *You are not trying hard enough. Get out there and meet someone.*

- *You don't really want to be married, or you would be.*

- *Your standards are much too high.*

- *I cannot believe you are getting a divorce. What did you do wrong?*

- *You did not try hard enough, or your marriage would have worked.*

- *You are much too picky.*

Comments from family can be very, very painful, and, unfortunately, no matter what you say, family members may not ever truly understand. How do you deal with the hurt and the misconceptions your family may place on you? You must simply walk in what God has shown you for today. Pray that God gives you the grace to love them despite any hurtful comments they may have made. Trust Him for your future!

I have been blessed with a family who is sympathetic concerning all my challenges with being single. They also seem to understand and believe that whatever God chooses for me is best. They have seen the joy, they have seen the sadness, but, thank God, they have seen the growth as I have learned contentment.

Misconceptions—everyone has them. It is highly possible that at some point during your life while you are single, people might think the following:

- *Something must be wrong with her or she would be married.*

- *She must have a hang-up about men.*

- *She is not trying hard enough, or she would be married.*

These are hurtful misconceptions. But what can you do about them? You can choose not to let them bother you. If you are doing everything to please the Lord, then it doesn't matter what people think. Make every effort to be your very best in every area of your life. Radiate God's goodness!

NOTE

1. David Popenoe, "Marriage Decline in America." Testimony. U.S. 107th Congress, 1st sess. H. Rpt. Washington, D.C.: GPO, 2001, p. 43.

The Real Prince
Is Coming

I was moved with emotion as I entered the room. The candles flickered and gave the perfect atmosphere to the dimly lit church. The flowers were magnificent, and the music was wonderful. The audience sat with great anticipation. Waiting. Soon the bride would come.

Weddings. I cannot begin to imagine how many I have attended in my life, but there have been a lot of them. Large, small, indoors, outdoors, extravagant, simple. . . . It seems there's always someone getting married. But this wedding, this church, these people, everything was picture perfect. The majority of those sitting around me were couples and families.

The longer I sat there, the harder it became. I had to fight the same question that I always have to guard myself from when I go to weddings—Why?

Tears began falling and I told myself, OK. *You are past*

this; you are fine. I wish I could tell you that because I am extremely happy being single I don't still have those moments, those times that can be difficult. It's not often that I do, but something about this wedding caused me to be emotional. Isn't that part of being a woman?

The groom entered the room, and we could see such joy on his face as he anticipated seeing his bride. Talk about handsome! After the entire wedding party had come in, it was time . . . time for the bride. As the music swelled, every person rose to his or her feet, looking, trying to see her face, her gown, her smile. She was one of the prettiest brides I had ever seen. Gorgeous. He was certainly tall, dark, and handsome, and she was blonde and beautiful.

They began saying their vows to each other, and I started trying to pull myself together a bit. "Will you love, honor, and cherish her?" What beautiful words. Oh, how we need husbands who will cherish their brides. *Cherish*— don't you love that word! We all would love to have someone to honor and cherish us.

How many young girls, how many women, are waiting, all hoping their prince will finally come to love and adore them? The Lord may choose to bring you a husband in the very near future. Is there still "a match made in heaven"? Oh, yes! God is still bringing couples together in miraculous ways, ways that only He can do. Does He have a match for you? Time will tell. Trust Him.

What if God does bring you a husband? Will he be perfect; will he meet your every desire? Certainly no one is perfect and life will have its set of challenges, whether you're married or single. If you are waiting on the perfect husband, please know there is just one.

The Real Prince Is on His Way

The real Prince is coming! Time is short; we don't know how long we will live. Each day that we have breath is a gift from the Lord. But so often we spend precious time dwelling on things that, in the end, will not really matter.

You may be thinking, *But I want flesh and blood. Someone I can see, someone I can touch, someone to laugh and cry with.* I understand. When life seems unbearable, simply not worth living, hold on. Don't think about tomorrow, next week, next month, or next year. The problems, the questions, the uncertainties of life can overwhelm us if we dwell on them. Focus on Him! This does not mean you do not need to plan or budget or make goals for your future. But God tells us:

> Do not be worried about your life, as to what you will eat or what you will drink; nor for your body, as to what you will put on. Is not life more than food, and the body more than clothing? Look at the birds of the air, that they do not sow, nor reap nor gather into barns, and yet your heavenly Father feeds them. Are you not worth much more than they? And who of you by being worried can add a single hour to his life? And why are you worried about clothing? (Matthew 6:25–28a)

The Lord Jesus Christ is my Husband. He truly takes care of me. This may sound so spiritual, so impersonal.

You may be thinking, *What does that really mean when I'm simply trying to live each day?*

Over and over again throughout my life, the Lord has taken care of me when I could not pick up a phone and call a husband. A number of years ago I had a car accident in a black convertible Fiat sports car. The canvas top had had its share of problems. While driving down the road, I tried reaching back to fix the top. Mistake. When I looked forward, I was headed toward the median. In order not to hit it, I pulled the steering wheel much too far in the other direction. My car spun completely around—in the middle of the interstate going about seventy miles an hour.

I thought my life might end that day. All I knew was to say, "God, help!" The back end of my car went off the side of the road, and it hit a mile-marker sign and stopped. This happened almost twenty years ago and, no, I was not wearing my seatbelt. I could not believe it. I did not have a bruise, a scratch . . . nothing. I was not hurt at all. I was never even sore. I got out of the car and all I could say was, "Thank You, Lord, thank You, Lord, thank You, Lord!"

Before I could even think about how I was going to get home (I was two hours away), a car pulled over. The couple in the car asked if I needed help and if they could take me somewhere. We called the wrecker service and had my car towed. The nice couple took me to my mother's home in Nashville. God knew just what I needed and when I needed it.

Whether it has been a broken heating unit during the Christmas holidays, a leaking water heater, a flat tire, or an unexpected bill, over and over again the Lord has provided.

He has been the Husband I have needed time and time again. He delights in meeting my every need. God says:

> Do not worry then, saying, "What will we eat?" or "What will we drink?" or "What will we wear for clothing?" For the Gentiles eagerly seek all these things; for your heavenly Father knows that you need all these things. But seek first His kingdom and His righteousness, and all these things will be added to you. So do not worry about tomorrow; for tomorrow will care for itself. Each day has enough trouble of its own. (Matthew 6:31–34)

Seek first His kingdom. This is what makes life worth living. If I focus on the Lord and the work of His kingdom, my problems seem insignificant. Nothing that is going on in our world is a surprise to God. I have heard people say about tragedy, "How can God allow such horrific things to take place?" He knows when lives are damaged by natural disasters, wars, or by the inhumane things people do to each other.

He Knows the Pain of This Life

My heart breaks when I think about the tragic events that took place on September 11, 2001. It is a day that no one will ever forget. It was like a dream, but it became our nightmare. America, the land of freedom and peace, shattered within a few brief moments. We stood at a crossroads and wondered how this ever could have happened.

Countless broken families now try to make sense out

of life—wives who no longer have husbands, husbands who no longer have wives, and children who don't have a mother or a daddy. You may have lost a boyfriend in a horrible accident, or someone who is very dear to you simply walked out of your life, and you don't know what you're going to do. You may feel like no one understands. But I know One who does. One who . . .

> for the joy set before Him endured the cross, despising the shame, and has sat down at the right hand of the throne of God. For consider Him who has endured such hostility by sinners against Himself, so that you will not grow weary and lose heart. You have not yet resisted to the point of shedding blood in your striving against sin. (Hebrews 12:2–4)

All your hurt, all your pain, pour out to Him. He understands.

> For we do not have a high priest who cannot sympathize with our weaknesses, but One who has been tempted in all things as we are, yet without sin. Therefore let us draw near with confidence to the throne of grace, so that we may receive mercy and may find grace to help in time of need. (Hebrews 4:15–16)

Feeling frightened, hurt, angry, and very alone? There is only one Husband whom you can always, always count on. He will never leave you. He will never forsake you. He will always love you. He knows what is best for you. You can trust Him with every single area of your life. He will listen when no one else will. He cares. He's your real Prince, Jesus Christ. He is coming. Do you ever wonder when?

God's Word says:

> For you yourselves know full well that the day of the Lord will come just like a thief in the night. While they are saying, "Peace and safety!" then destruction will come upon them suddenly like labor pains upon a woman with child, and they will not escape. But you, brethren, are not in darkness, that the day would overtake you like a thief; for you are all sons of light and sons of day. We are not of night nor of darkness; so then let us not sleep as others do, but let us be alert and sober. (1 Thessalonians 5:2–6)

We may not know the time of His return, but we're to always be ready. Does it seem like our world is changing? The Middle East crisis, 9-11, the crazy weather, suicide bombers . . . with all of this madness, do you wonder, *What is going on?* I am amazed when I hear even some of our news commentators mention Armageddon. It's as though everyone senses we are living in unprecedented times.

We could live in great fear and disbelief that anything good could come from all the craziness and wonder, *Does anyone have an answer to all of this?* Praise God, He has the answers. He tells us in His Word how the end will be:

> But realize this, that in the last days difficult times will come. For men will be lovers of self, lovers of money, boastful, arrogant, revilers, disobedient to parents, ungrateful,

unholy, unloving, irreconcilable, malicious gossips, without self-control, brutal, haters of good, treacherous, reckless, conceited, lovers of pleasure rather than lovers of God, holding to a form of godliness, although they have denied its power; Avoid such men as these. For among them are those who enter into households and captivate weak women weighed down with sins, led on by various impulses, always learning and never able to come to the knowledge of the truth. (2 Timothy 3:1–7)

Does this sound like our world today? Unfortunately, it seems to describe it perfectly. Who would have ever thought that we would see our children shooting each other? As if Columbine weren't enough, the killing continues. We seem to be, as the Scripture says, "without self-control." We have a form of godliness without the power of true godliness . . . We're always learning and never coming to the knowledge of the truth (2 Timothy 3:3, 5, 7).

It may appear our world is going mad. Everyone seems to be saying, "God bless America," but at times I wonder, *What are we asking for; what blessings are we looking for?* Do we want financial blessings, family blessings, or should we desire His favor?

Our greatest desire should not be for money, a husband, or children, but to be in the center of His will. There is no better place on earth than being right in the palm of His hand.

Certainly there is nothing wrong with having some of these desires. But we should want His desires over ours. Will I ever get married? Only God knows. But my future does hold a wedding—a wedding unlike one that anyone has ever seen.

Be Ready for Your Wedding Day

In the book of Revelation we read about the greatest wedding that will ever take place.

> Then I heard something like the voice of a great multitude and like the sound of many waters and like the sound of mighty peals of thunder, saying, "Hallelujah! For the Lord our God, the Almighty, reigns. Let us rejoice and be glad and give the glory to Him, for the marriage of the Lamb has come and His bride has made herself ready." It was given to her to clothe herself in fine linen, bright and clean; for the fine linen is the righteous acts of the saints. Then he said to me, "Write, 'Blessed are those who are invited to the marriage supper of the Lamb.'" (Revelation 19:6–9)

I have never seen a bride who didn't get ready for her wedding. All the shopping, all the searching, all the decisions: choosing the perfect gown, the tuxedos, the bridesmaid dresses, the rings, and the flowers. I had an acquaintance who would come in to work and say, "Well, just 365 days left until my wedding . . . just 364 days until my wedding . . . 363 days until my wedding." I heard this all year long. She was cute, and this is how excited every bride should be.

Are you getting ready? He tells us to be prepared. There is nothing like a long white wedding dress. I have seen some dresses that were almost breathtaking, but the finest gown in all the world will not compare to how we will be dressed for Christ's return. "Excited" doesn't begin to describe it.

The Amplified Bible describes it this way:

Let us rejoice and shout for joy [exulting and triumphant]! Let us celebrate and ascribe to Him glory and honor, for the marriage of the Lamb [at last] has come, and His bride has prepared herself. She has been permitted to dress in fine (radiant) linen, dazzling and white—for the fine linen is (signifies, represents) the righteousness (the up right, just, and godly living, deeds, and conduct, and right standing with God) of the saints (God's holy people). (Revelation 19:7–8, brackets in original)

What an awesome description of the bride. Yes, most women desire to become earthly brides. This is normal. But, above all else, we should long to be His bride, dressed "in fine (radiant) linen," signifying our righteousness, being in right standing with Him, having conducted our lives in godly living, God's holy people. Does this describe your life?

What will the Bridegroom be like? Revelation goes on to say:

Then I fell at his [the angel's] feet to worship him. But he said to me, "Do not do that; I am a fellow servant of yours and your brethren who hold the testimony of Jesus; worship God. For the testimony of Jesus is the spirit of prophecy."

And I saw heaven opened, and behold, a white horse, and He who sat on it is called Faithful and True, and in righteousness He judges and wages war. His eyes are a flame of fire, and on His head are many diadems; and He has a name written on Him which no one knows except Himself. He is clothed with a robe dipped in blood, and His name is called The Word of God. And the armies which are in heaven, clothed in fine linen, white and clean, were following Him on white horses. From His mouth comes a sharp sword, so that with it He may strike down the nations, and He will rule them with a rod of iron; and He treads the wine press of the fierce wrath of God, the Almighty. And on His robe and on His thigh He has a name written, "KING OF KINGS, AND LORD OF LORDS." (Revelation 19:10–16)

The real Prince is coming. I hope you have made Him your King, your Lord. I wish I could tell you that God is going to bring you a husband, but I can't. He certainly will if this is part of His plan for your life. While you're waiting, get ready for the greatest Bridegroom there ever will be. His love is beyond your wildest dreams. His grace and mercy never end. His unfailing love will forever sustain you and give you a hope. You will have eternal life, and that is greater than anything in this world. Heaven is our real home.

Then I saw a new heaven and a new earth; for the first heaven and the first earth passed away, and there is no longer any sea. And I saw the holy city, new Jerusalem, coming down out of heaven from God, made ready as a bride adorned for her husband. And I heard a loud voice from the throne, saying, "Behold, the tabernacle of God is among men, and He will dwell among them, and they shall be His people, and God Himself will be among them, and He will wipe away every tear from their eyes; and there will no longer be any death; there will no longer be any mourning, or crying, or pain; the first things have passed away." And He who sits on the throne said, "Behold, I am making all things new." And He said, "Write, for these words are faithful and true." Then He said to me, "It is done. I am the Alpha and the Omega, the beginning and the end." (Revelation 21:1–6)

I often stand amazed at people who wait so late in life to ever start thinking about eternity. Our souls are eternal, without end. This life is short, but we often get wrapped up in the here and now. Many spend their lives getting ready for this life, when we need to spend our lives preparing for eternity. Not that you don't live—yes, you live, but you live with every ounce of your being knowing why you're here.

In his book called *Eternity*, Joseph Stowell says,

Life is most disappointing, most despairing, when it is lived as though this world is all we have. Questions have few answers, and crises become all-consuming. Thankfully, this is not the only world. Christ connects us to the eternal world to come and provides for us an eternally redeemed world within. This present world makes sense only when we live here in light of these other worlds.[1]

As Paul said, "If we have hoped in Christ in this life only, we are of all men most to be pitied" (1 Corinthians 15:19).

Too often people wait much too late in life before they finally begin asking the important questions. *Where did I come from? Why am I here? What is my purpose? Where am I going after I die? What is real happiness?* Single or married, everyone is searching. Praise God, it is never too late to find the answers.

Are you waiting for a prince, hoping he can give you the answers to life and the happiness you have been waiting for . . . then you can finally have peace? Isn't that what every woman is looking for?

I enjoy watching Barbara Walters specials. It fascinates me to see scores of bright, intelligent, gifted, wonderful people . . . so many still searching, still trying to find the "something missing" in their lives. It's as if Barbara tries to reach down into their souls to see what really makes them tick. As if trying to find out what gives them joy, what brings them heartache, she asks the almost-certain question, "Do you have peace?"

My friend, do you lack peace today because your prince hasn't come? Hold on—the greatest Prince who will ever be is coming. He is the Prince of peace. He is the truest source of joy in all the world. Keep waiting. Keep trusting. Keep believing that Jesus Christ will come to take His bride. Are you ready?

"His name will be called Wonderful Counselor, Mighty God, Eternal Father, Prince of Peace" (Isaiah 9:6).

NOTE

1. Joseph M. Stowell, *Eternity: Reclaiming a Passion for What Endures* (Chicago: Moody, 1995), 13.

Moody Press, a ministry of Moody Bible Institute,
is designed for education, evangelization, and edification.
If we may assist you in knowing more about Christ
and the Christian life, please write us without obligation:
Moody Press, c/o MLM, Chicago, Illinois 60610.